# CONTENTS

Page

## WITNESSES



## LETTERS, STATEMENTS, ETC., SUBMITTED FOR THE HEARING

# OFFSHORE BANKING, CORRUPTION, AND THE WAR ON TERRORISM

---

# HEARING

BEFORE THE

## SUBCOMMITTEE ON OVERSIGHT AND INVESTIGATIONS

OF THE

## COMMITTEE ON INTERNATIONAL RELATIONS HOUSE OF REPRESENTATIVES

ONE HUNDRED NINTH CONGRESS

SECOND SESSION

---

MARCH 29, 2006

---

**Serial No. 109–154**

---

Printed for the use of the Committee on International Relations

Available via the World Wide Web: http://www.house.gov/international_relations

---

U.S. GOVERNMENT PRINTING OFFICE

26–777PDF WASHINGTON : 2006

For sale by the Superintendent of Documents, U.S. Government Printing Office
Internet: bookstore.gpo.gov Phone: toll free (866) 512–1800; DC area (202) 512–1800
Fax: (202) 512–2250 Mail: Stop SSOP, Washington, DC 20402–0001

## COMMITTEE ON INTERNATIONAL RELATIONS

HENRY J. HYDE, Illinois, *Chairman*

JAMES A. LEACH, Iowa
CHRISTOPHER H. SMITH, New Jersey, *Vice Chairman*
DAN BURTON, Indiana
ELTON GALLEGLY, California
ILEANA ROS-LEHTINEN, Florida
DANA ROHRABACHER, California
EDWARD R. ROYCE, California
PETER T. KING, New York
STEVE CHABOT, Ohio
THOMAS G. TANCREDO, Colorado
RON PAUL, Texas
DARRELL ISSA, California
JEFF FLAKE, Arizona
JO ANN DAVIS, Virginia
MARK GREEN, Wisconsin
JERRY WELLER, Illinois
MIKE PENCE, Indiana
THADDEUS G. McCOTTER, Michigan
KATHERINE HARRIS, Florida
JOE WILSON, South Carolina
JOHN BOOZMAN, Arkansas
J. GRESHAM BARRETT, South Carolina
CONNIE MACK, Florida
JEFF FORTENBERRY, Nebraska
MICHAEL McCAUL, Texas
TED POE, Texas

TOM LANTOS, California
HOWARD L. BERMAN, California
GARY L. ACKERMAN, New York
ENI F.H. FALEOMAVAEGA, American Samoa
DONALD M. PAYNE, New Jersey
SHERROD BROWN, Ohio
BRAD SHERMAN, California
ROBERT WEXLER, Florida
ELIOT L. ENGEL, New York
WILLIAM D. DELAHUNT, Massachusetts
GREGORY W. MEEKS, New York
BARBARA LEE, California
JOSEPH CROWLEY, New York
EARL BLUMENAUER, Oregon
SHELLEY BERKLEY, Nevada
GRACE F. NAPOLITANO, California
ADAM B. SCHIFF, California
DIANE E. WATSON, California
ADAM SMITH, Washington
BETTY McCOLLUM, Minnesota
BEN CHANDLER, Kentucky
DENNIS A. CARDOZA, California
RUSS CARNAHAN, Missouri

THOMAS E. MOONEY, SR., *Staff Director/General Counsel*
ROBERT R. KING, *Democratic Staff Director*

---

## SUBCOMMITTEE ON OVERSIGHT AND INVESTIGATIONS

DANA ROHRABACHER, California, *Chairman*

EDWARD R. ROYCE, California
JEFF FLAKE, Arizona, *Vice Chairman*
MARK GREEN, Wisconsin
MIKE PENCE, Indiana
JOE WILSON, South Carolina

WILLIAM D. DELAHUNT, Massachusetts
HOWARD L. BERMAN, California
BETTY McCOLLUM, Minnesota
ADAM B. SCHIFF, California

GREGG RICKMAN, *Subcommittee Staff Director*
GREGORY McCARTHY, *Professional Staff Member*
CLIFF STAMMERMAN, *Democratic Professional Staff Member*
EMILY ANDERSON, *Staff Associate*

# OFFSHORE BANKING, CORRUPTION, AND THE WAR ON TERRORISM

**WEDNESDAY, MARCH 29, 2006**

HOUSE OF REPRESENTATIVES,
SUBCOMMITTEE ON OVERSIGHT AND INVESTIGATIONS,
COMMITTEE ON INTERNATIONAL RELATIONS,
*Washington, DC.*

The Subcommittee met, pursuant to notice, at 2:04 p.m. in Room 2200, Rayburn House Office Building, Hon. Dana Rohrabacher (Chairman of the Subcommittee) presiding.

Mr. ROHRABACHER. This hearing of the Oversight and Investigations Subcommittee is called to order.

We are convening this hearing of the Oversight and Investigations Subcommittee to discuss the role of banking institutions, especially international banking institutions, and their connection to corruption and the war on terror.

We have all heard about the existence of banks operating in Switzerland and in the Caribbean and that these banks perhaps cater to companies and people seeing to avoid taxes. Yet, the same system also makes it possible for drug lords and even terrorists to do their business.

This Subcommittee's recent investigation into the United Nations showed how one corrupt procurement officer, an Alexander Yakovlev, was able to hide at least $1 million in an offshore bank in Antigua. He was not alone, however. According to the Bank of International Settlements, which is essentially the central bank of central banks from all over the world, it is estimated that in 2004, there was some $2.7 trillion in offshore accounts. Now, that is trillion with a T and not with a B, not billions, but trillions of dollars.

While I would like to believe that this money largely comprises funds from tax cheats or even people who maybe feel they are overtaxed, it seems more logical to believe that as Raymond Baker and Jennifer Nordin wrote in the *Financial Times* last October, and I quote: "It is virtually impossible to do business using tax havens, secrecy, and secret jurisdictions without abusing transfer pricing and using anonymous entities and secret accounts," and, here it is, "without breaking laws and perpetrating injustices in many countries."

So offshore banking involves methods by which money can be purposely hidden and transferred and then, as has long been the case, used for illegal and even violent purposes.

Not only people and companies use these institutions to obtain safe haven for their assets, but countries use these vehicles and the leaders of countries use these vehicles and, I might say, countries and leaders who are under United States sanction use these vehicles. They use these banks for their own purposes as well as to just evade sanctions.

In this first hearing on the corrosive nature of offshore banking, we want to not only learn how these banks operate and how the bad guys get away with these transactions, but also how these institutions work against the United States by aiding countries and, yes, even terrorists, who oppose us.

In this instance, I want to briefly discuss the role of the Swiss bank UBS, or the United Bank of Switzerland. Swiss banks have long been known for their bank secrecy. More recently, however, what comes to mind when one discusses the Swiss banks' corruption and duplicity, is the role in withholding assets, for example, of the Holocaust victims and their heirs for over a half a century.

UBS is one of the Swiss banks that settled a class action lawsuit against Swiss banks with the survivors of the Holocaust for $1.25 billion in 1998.

Since this time, we have heard other stories of UBS malfeasance, including U.S. regulatory fines, lawsuits and other accusations of impropriety, including the fact that UBS once held an account for none other than Osama Bin Laden.

What concerns us greatly is the role UBS has played in not only supplying United States dollar bank notes to Iran several years ago as part of the Extended Custody Inventory program, or the ECI program, but also their reasons for doing this. The ECI program serves as a means to facilitate the international distribution of U.S. bank notes and the return of old design bank notes and to strengthen U.S. information gathering on the use of U.S. currency and the source of counterfeiting and the use of counterfeit U.S. currency abroad.

According to UBS, over $440 million in United States bank notes was supplied to Iran during the 1990s and beyond that through the ECI program. This was in total contravention to the United States sanctions on Iran. We need to know about that.

What concerns us is the motivation for supplying this money to Iran against the directions of the ECI program. Was UBS worrying about other business that it had with Iran? Did those in the bank think that supplying these bank notes would help in that business? So were they sacrificing the interests of the United States for very parochial interests on their part?

Iran at time was facing a credit crunch by the United States as we attempted to prevent international investment in Iran's energy sector. I believe, of course, the targets and the goals set out by the United States were legitimate goals, and we can see even to this day that the failure of achieving our goals with Iran through some economic pressure like this—the fact that that did not work—they put the whole world in jeopardy, when a radical regime like that exists in Iran in possession of nuclear weapons. A grave threat that might be traced right back to a major financial institution in the world dealing with the Iranian Government in a way that contradicts an understanding with the United States Government.

If the United States was trying to restrict Iran's flow of income but UBS was working to supplement it through loans and credit, then it seems to me that the bank, which has a substantial presence here in the United States, was working directly against the interests of our country and, yes, the interests of a safer and more stable world.

It seems to me that if we are going to permit banks to operate freely and they are having that type of negative impact, we need a second look at the whole premise of our relationship with the world financial institutions like UBS.

To make matters worse, when UBS then transferred United States bank notes to Iran in violation of the very program that they were entrusted to run, I should state that UBS was indeed fined $100 million by the United States Government for these violations. We are, however, interested in learning about the bank's role in opposing United States efforts to restrict Iran's flow of income and why they took the extraordinary effort to illicitly transfer bank notes to that country in the first place.

Today, we have a number of prominent practitioners in the field of anti-corruption who deal with banking institutions around the world and they will discuss not only the UBS problem but how banks do business in hiding the wealth of dictators, drug dealers, and others threatening the financial well being of our country and the peace of the world and how they are helping others actually make their profit through corruption—you might say accomplices in what should be considered criminal activity.

When dictators like Mobuti, Duvalier and others raid the wealth of their countries and hide it in respected financial institutions, then these banks end up treating the money like it belongs to them, which is bad for the people who it was stolen from—the dictator stole it from somebody—but it is bad for the entire world and undermines any efforts to try to bring the third world up to a level of prosperity so their people can live a decent standard of living. It is a horrendous crime.

These practices must end and the first thing we do to try to end it is to shed some light on the issue, and this is the first in a series of hearings that we will hold on international financial institutions, finding out how they operate, what their motives are and whether or not we need to rein in some of these practices that I just mentioned.

I will now turn to my friend and Ranking Member, Mr. Delahunt, if he has a statement to make.

[The prepared statement of Mr. Rohrabacher follows:]

PREPARED STATEMENT OF THE HONORABLE DANA ROHRABACHER, A REPRESENTATIVE IN CONGRESS FROM THE STATE OF CALIFORNIA, AND CHAIRMAN, SUBCOMMITTEE ON OVERSIGHT AND INVESTIGATIONS

We are convening this hearing of the Oversight & Investigations Subcommittee to discuss the role of banking institutions and their connection to corruption and the war on terrorism.

We have all heard of the existence of banks operating in Switzerland and the Caribbean that cater to companies and people seeking to avoid taxes. Yet, this same system also makes it possible for drug lords and even terrorists to thrive.

This subcommittee's recent investigation into the United Nations showed how one corrupt procurement officer, Alexander Yakovlev, was able to hide at least $1 million in an offshore bank in Antigua.

Mr. Yakovlev was not alone, however. According to the Bank for International Settlements, which is essentially the Central Bank of Central Banks from all over the world, it is estimated that in 2004 there was some $2.7 TRILLION in offshore accounts—that's TRILLION, *not Billion*.

While I would like to believe that this money largely comprises funds from tax cheats, it seems more logical to believe that as Raymond Baker and Jennifer Nordin wrote in the *Financial Times* last October, "It is virtually impossible to do business using tax havens, secrecy jurisdictions, abuse transfer pricing, anonymous entities and secret accounts *without breaking laws and perpetrating injustices* in many countries."

Offshore banking involves methods by which money can be purposely hidden and transferred and then, as has long been the case, used for illegal and even violent purposes. Not only people and companies use these institutions to obtain safe haven for their assets, but countries—even countries under US sanctions—use these banking institutions as well for purposes of sanctions evasion.

In this first hearing on the corrosive nature of offshore banking, we want to not only learn how these banks operate and how the bad guys get away with these transactions, but also how these institutions work against United States by aiding countries that oppose us.

In this instance, I want to briefly discuss the role of the Swiss Bank, UBS or the United Bank of Switzerland. Swiss banks have long been known for their bank secrecy. More recently, however, what comes to mind when one discusses the Swiss banks corruption and duplicity. When I speak of this, I speak of their role in withholding the assets of Holocaust victims and their heirs for over half-a-century. UBS was one of the Swiss banks that settled a class-action lawsuit against Swiss banks with the survivors for *$1.25 billion* in 1998.

Since this time, we have heard other stories of UBS' malfeasance including US regulatory fines, lawsuits, and other accusations of impropriety including the fact that UBS once held an account for Osama Bin Laden.

But what concerns us greatly is the role UBS played in not only supplying US dollar banknotes to Iran several years ago as part of the Extended Custodial Inventory program or ECI program, but also their reasons for doing so. The ECI program serves as a means to facilitate the international distribution of U.S. banknotes and the return of old design banknotes and to strengthen U.S. information gathering on the use of U.S. currency and sources of counterfeiting of U.S. currency abroad.

According to UBS, over $440 million in US banknotes was supplied to Iran during the 1990s and beyond through the ECI program in contravention of US sanctions on Iran.

What concerns us is the motivation for supplying this money against the directions of the ECI program. Was UBS worrying about other business that it had with Iran and did those in the bank think that supplying these banknotes would help that business?

Iran at that time was facing a credit crunch by the US as we attempted to prevent international investment in Iran's energy sector. If the US was trying to restrict Iran's flow of income, but UBS was working to supplement it through loans and credit, then it seems to me that the bank which has a substantial presence here in the US was working *directly* against the interests of the country that acted as one of its most important sources of business.

To make matters worse, UBS then transferred US banknotes to Iran in violation of the very program they were entrusted to run. I should state that UBS was indeed fined $100 million by the US government for these violations. We are however interested in learning of the banks' role in opposing US efforts to restrict Iran's flow of income and why they took the extraordinary effort to illicitly transfer banknotes to that country.

Today we have a number of prominent practitioners in the field of anti-corruption who deal with banking institutions around the world and they will discuss not only the UBS problem, but how banks do business in hiding the wealth of dictators, drug dealers and others threatening the financial well-being of our country and others through this corruption. When dictators like Mobutu, Duvalier, Abacha, and others raid the wealth of their countries and hide it in these banks, the banks then treat the money like it belongs to them, not the people the dictator stole it from. These practices must end

I now turn to my friend the Ranking Member, Mr. Delahunt to make his statement.

Mr. DELAHUNT. Yes. I am going to be very brief, Mr. Chairman.

Let me just make an observation that you have heard at just about every hearing. This Congress, between a variety of Subcommittees, has held numerous hearings on the UN, on the UN Oil-for-Food program, and today we are having a hearing on a Swiss bank, even though there have been several hearings in front of the Financial Services Committee on this particular matter. It was investigated by Federal law enforcement and by Swiss authorities and the Chair is correct in terms of the sanction that was imposed on UBS. The matter was settled and that is good.

We do have much to learn, but I think it is fascinating that we are unable to have hearings relative to reports of corruption and possible illegal activity when it comes to matters that might cause some embarrassment to the Administration.

Media reports, for example, over the past several years have raised serious questions about the propriety of business dealings by Halliburton's wholly-owned subsidiary, Halliburton Products and Services, that they conducted with Iran.

The Chairman mentioned Iran and I remember watching a *60 Minutes* report that I found rather shocking. In fact, the Department of Justice (DOJ) has initiated grand jury investigations into whether the subsidiary's activities have violated U.S. sanctions laws.

Now, I recognize that Halliburton Products and Services is nominally incorporated in the Cayman Islands. I think it is fair to say that the Cayman Islands is an OFC (Offshore Financial Haven) or a tax haven. However, according to the media report that I alluded to, the registered address of the subsidiary was located in a building owned by the local Caledonian Bank. However, according to the manager of that bank, there actually is no office for the company there, just a mail box, and that he forwards mail that is addressed there directly to Halliburton's Houston headquarters.

I suggest that this calls into question the legal requirement that a subsidiary operate independently of its U.S. parent.

I am glad to hear, Mr. Chairman, that we are going to have additional hearings on this issue and I would hope that we could invite members of the Halliburton Corporation and its subsidiary before this Subcommittee to examine its conduct. I think some balance is necessary here. We just simply cannot ignore the realities and continue to focus on issues that assuredly will not prove to be an embarrassment for the Administration.

So with that, I will conclude, and I look forward—I did read the testimony. I found it interesting and insightful. I noted that two of the individuals, Mr. Moscow and Mr. Middlemiss, work for the District Attorney in Manhattan. Mr. Morgenthau, whom I had occasion to interact with during my previous career—I have great respect for Mr. Morgenthau and he clearly was a leader in terms of dealing with the issues that we are concerned about and deserves great credit and, I would suggest, could serve as a role model for some of our Federal agencies.

With that, I will yield back.

Mr. ROHRABACHER. Thank you very much.

Ms. Ros-Lehtinen?

Ms. ROS-LEHTINEN. Thank you so much.

I thank Chairman Rohrabacher for the opportunity to participate in today's Subcommittee hearing. The timing could not have been more appropriate, as it comes on the heels of the Full Committee's adoption of my Iran sanctions legislation, House Resolution 282, that is co-sponsored by 356 Members of Congress and it underscores the commitment of the United States Congress to deny the regime in Iran the resources to engage in state sponsorship of global terrorism and to continue to develop its chemical, biological and nuclear weapons program.

So it is therefore incumbent upon this Committee and all of us in Congress to investigate the activities of financial institutions and assess whether they are assisting the war on terrorism or in some instances are enabling jihad of the individuals or groups or state sponsors of terrorism who seek our destruction.

I am particularly interested in hearing from Mr. Michael Herde of UBS regarding what he states is the bank's highest priority, to be a strong ally in the fight against money laundering and terrorist financing.

My experience with UBS in the last few years regarding UBS's transactions with terrorist regimes under the Extended Custodial Inventory program calls into question the extent of the bank's stated commitment to fight terrorist financing. However, I will go back to the ECI transactions in a second.

I would hope that Mr. Herde would elaborate on the indicators that UBS uses to determine if money laundering and terrorist financing is taking place, what preventative safeguards are in place, and what corrective actions are taken to immediately shut down UBS as a vehicle for such activity.

Mr. Herde's written testimony says that UBS's new policy tracks economic sanctions imposed by the United States, Switzerland, the EU (European Union) and the UN Security Council, so if an individual entity or government is subject to U.S. sanctions but not UN Security Council sanctions, which one would UBS use to determine how to proceed? For example, if Iran's so-called President sought to deposit funds in a UBS account and sought to use UBS services, what would be the response of UBS?

Turning to another brutal dictator and state sponsor of terrorism, if Fidel Castro were to seek UBS services, what response should he expect?

Does Castro or any other Cuban official agency or instrumentality of the Cuban regime currently have accounts in UBS?

In information provided by UBS to the Subcommittee, UBS states that it is ending all other—that is, beyond ECI—business dealings with a limited number of countries, including Iran. The information then says, "Except for transactions permitted" for such certain international organizations like the UN.

I hope that the witness would elaborate on the extent of UBS's previous and current transactions with Iran, China, North Korea, or any other country designated the United States as a state sponsor of terrorism. What about officials and entities of these regimes?

Reports have stated that Saddam Hussein, even when Iraq was under UN sanctions, had accounts in UBS. This has implications for this Subcommittee's Oil-for-Food investigation.

As you know, Mr. Rohrabacher, I have been following the issues we are discussing today for several years now and my interest was reinvigorated in April 2003 when a United States Army sergeant broke through a false wall in a building in Iraq and discovered more than $600 million in new United States currency. The Federal Reserve and the Department of Treasury determined that through the Extended Custodial Inventory (ECI) program, UBS had engaged in billions of dollars worth of transactions with terrorist regimes and sanctioned countries, including Cuba and Iran; this in clear violation of United States laws.

Of the $5 billion in total transactions among all entities subject to U.S. sanctions, $5 billion, $3.9 billion worth of U.S. currency went to the Castro regime.

Since June 2004, some of my colleagues and I have been meeting with and writing to UBS officials to ascertain the extent of the bank's dealing with the Cuban dictatorship and any possible linkages between the Cuban and Iranian counterparties. Some of the questions posed were, for example, was the account of the Cuban counterparty involved in the transaction with UBS permanently closed and, if so, where are the funds that were in that account?

Did the funds remain at UBS or were they transferred to other banks?

Were these foreign banks, and, if so, where are they headquartered?

What was the pattern of activity of the account? Were there any spikes in activity and for what purpose?

Was there any interaction between the Cuban and Iranian counterparties?

The latter is particularly relevant, given the joint statements made by Iran's Grand Ayatollah and Castro in the summer of 2001, declaring their commitment to "bring American to its knees."

It is particularly relevant given the growing relationship between the two regimes across multiple sectors, yet beyond just general apologies and assurances from UBS to trust that the ECI violations were an isolated incident, our requests were essentially ignored.

As President Ronald Reagan said, "Trust but verify."

I would like to have, Mr. Chairman, my correspondence with UBS on these matters included in the record of today's hearing and ask the Subcommittee's assistance in securing the responses and documentation from UBS relating to these.

Mr. ROHRABACHER. Without objection, that will be placed in the record and the Subcommittee staff will be at your service to pursue the answers to those questions.

[The information referred to follows:]

DEPARTMENT OF THE TREASURY
WASHINGTON, D.C. 20220

JAN - 6 2005

FAC No. MUL-236964

The Honorable Ileana Ros-Lehtinen
U. S. House of Representatives
Washington, D.C. 20515

Dear Ms. Ros-Lehtinen:

Thank you for your letter to Secretary Snow, dated November 30, 2004. I hope that you have now received our reply to your October 29 letter to Secretary Snow concerning the Extended Custodial Inventory ("ECI") program of the Federal Reserve Banks. I have enclosed a copy with this response for your reference.

We appreciate your continued interest in the trading of banknotes and your request that OFAC study whether or not Cuba and Iran had any links with each other concerning banknote trading.

Funds in accounts under U.S. jurisdiction in which there is an interest of the government of Cuba or a Cuban national are required to be blocked under the Cuban Assets Control Regulations by operation of law. Regarding possible violations of the Trading with the Enemy Act or the International Emergency Economic Powers Act, with respect to Cuba, if it is found that a person subject to U.S. jurisdiction is involved, appropriate action will be taken. Under the Iranian Transactions Regulations, there are no blocking provisions. As we did with the October 29 letter, we have taken the liberty of sharing your November 30 letter with officials who have direct investigative responsibility for the matter.

If you have any questions, please call OFAC's Congressional Liaison, Daniel Yorks, at 202-622-1663.

Sincerely,

Robert W. Werner
Director
Office of Foreign Assets Control

Enclosure

COMMITTEES:
INTERNATIONAL RELATIONS
GOVERNMENT REFORM
CHAIR:
SUBCOMMITTEE ON
MIDDLE EAST
AND CENTRAL ASIA
VICE CHAIR:
SUBCOMMITTEE ON
WESTERN HEMISPHERE
SUBCOMMITTEE ON
WELLNESS AND
HUMAN RIGHTS

**Congress of the United States**
**House of Representatives**
ILEANA ROS-LEHTINEN
18TH DISTRICT, FLORIDA

PLEASE RESPOND TO:
2160 RAYBURN HOUSE OFFICE BUILDING
WASHINGTON, DC 20515-0918
(202) 225-3931
FAX: (202) 225-5620

DISTRICT OFFICE:
9210 SUNSET DRIVE
SUITE 100
MIAMI, FL 33173
(305) 275-1800
FAX: (305) 275-1801

November 30, 2004

The Honorable John W. Snow
Secretary
U.S. Department of the Treasury
1500 Pennsylvania Avenue, N.W.
Washington, D.C. 20520

Dear Secretary Snow:

A month ago, in a letter dated October 29th, I wrote to you to follow-up on previous inquiries relating to the billions of dollars worth of transactions between UBS and the terrorist regimes in Cuba and Iran, through the Extended Custodial Inventory (ECI) program, in violation of U.S. laws. (See attached letter.)

On a related matter, I respectfully request that Treasury also look at the history of the Cuban and Iranian accounts and ascertain any possible linkages between the two, the nature of their activities, and the current status of the accounts.

Further, since the ECI deposits to the Cuban and Iranian accounts in UBS were illegally obtained, Treasury should consider seeking to seize the funds in these accounts in an amount equal to the total value of the illegal transactions--an amount close to $5 billion.

I look forward to receiving an update on these issues in the near future.

Thank you for your assistance and cooperation.

Sincerely,

Ileana Ros-Lehtinen
Member of Congress

cc: The Honorable Henry J. Hyde, Chairman
Committee on International Relations

UBS

UBS AG
Financial Services Group
P.O. Box
CH-8098 Zurich
Tel. +41-1-234 11 11

Peter Kurer
Group General Counsel
Member of the Group Executive Board

Bahnhofstrasse 45, 8001 Zürich
Tel. +41-1-234 45 47
Fax +41-1-234 88 55
peter.kurer@ubs.com

www.ubs.com

The Honorable Ileana Ros-Lehtinen
2160 Rayburn House Office Building
U.S. House of Representatives
Washington, D.C. 20515

November 4, 2004

Dear Congresswoman Ros-Lehtinen

Thank you for your letter of October 13 to our chairman, Marcel Ospel, regarding UBS's past participation in the Federal Reserve's Extended Custodial Inventory program.

The business area responsible for our relationship with the program was the UBS Investment Bank. We have asked Senator Phil Gramm, who is a Vice Chairman of UBS Investment Bank, and David Aufhauser, who has joined as the Global General Counsel of the Investment Bank, to arrange a meeting with you to further discuss your concerns.

We have taken a number of steps to demonstrate that we are a leader among international banks in ensuring the integrity of the international payment system. My colleagues can also review those steps with you. I was pleased to hear that your July meeting with our representatives was useful.

Sincerely,

Peter Kurer

cc: Marcel Ospel
Peter Wuffli

DEPARTMENT OF THE TREASURY
WASHINGTON, D.C. 20020

DEC - 3 2004

FAC No. MUL-235400

The Honorable Ileana Ros-Lehtinen
U. S. House of Representatives
Washington, D.C. 20515

Dear Ms. Ros-Lehtinen:

Thank you for your letter to Secretary Snow, dated October 29, 2004, and your continued interest in the movement of U.S. dollars to and from sanctioned countries, such as Cuba and Iran, by way of the Extended Custodial Inventory ("ECI") program of the Federal Reserve Banks.

While OFAC has responsibility for civil enforcement, we look to federal law enforcement agencies to conduct criminal investigations of the sanctions programs that we administer and have done so in this case. We have taken the liberty of sharing your October 29 letter with officials who have direct investigative responsibility for the matter.

Separate from the issue of an investigation into possible violations of the Trading with the Enemy Act or the International Emergency Economic Powers Act, OFAC will study the information you provided in your letter for any other appropriate enforcement actions that fall within our jurisdiction.

Regarding the currency serial numbers, UBS did not track the numbers of outgoing banknotes during the time the transactions took place. Therefore, tracking their whereabouts is problematic. We have been informed that the institutions currently functioning as ECIs are now "seized of the issue." At least one of them is now scanning serial numbers on all outgoing bundles of banknotes being delivered to counterparties, and all ECIs are looking into appropriate technology for their individual systems that would allow them to do tracking.

If you have any questions, please call me at 202-622-2500.

Sincerely,

Robert W. Werner
Director
Office of Foreign Assets Control

COMMITTEES:
INTERNATIONAL RELATIONS
GOVERNMENT REFORM
CHAIR:
SUBCOMMITTEE ON MIDDLE EAST AND CENTRAL ASIA
VICE CHAIR:
SUBCOMMITTEE ON WESTERN HEMISPHERE
SUBCOMMITTEE ON WELLNESS AND HUMAN RIGHTS

**Congress of the United States**
**House of Representatives**

ILEANA ROS-LEHTINEN
18TH DISTRICT, FLORIDA

PLEASE RESPOND TO:
2160 RAYBURN HOUSE OFFICE BUILDING
WASHINGTON, DC 20515-0918
(202) 225-3931
FAX: (202) 225-5620

DISTRICT OFFICE:
9210 SUNSET DRIVE
SUITE 100
MIAMI, FL 33173
(305) 275-1800
FAX: (305) 275-1801

October 29, 2004

The Honorable John W. Snow
Secretary
U.S. Department of the Treasury
1500 Pennsylvania Avenue, N.W.
Washington, D.C. 20520

Dear Secretary Snow:

I am writing to follow-up on previous inquiries relating to the billions of dollars worth of transactions between UBS and the terrorist regimes in Cuba and Iran, through the Extended Custodial Inventory (ECI) program, in violation of U.S. laws.

I have received information from sources familiar with the Castro regime's global financial network which indicate that, in addition to UBS, the Cuban dictatorship may have used or could be using, the following international institutions to undertake financial transactions in dollars it may not want monitored or tracked back to Cuban officials. These institutions are: Credit Suisse (Switzerland); CIBC (Canada); Barclays (UK); Bank von Ernst (UK); Banco Sabdell y BBVA (Spain); and Grupo Financieros BANAMEX y BANCOMER (Mexico).

I respectfully request, as part of your investigation into UBS' or other ECI banks' activities with Cuba—a state-sponsor of terrorism-- and, more broadly, as part of Treasury's terrorist financing efforts, you also look into these banking institutions.

Secondly, I ask you secure the serial numbers of the currency provided by UBS to the Cuban and Iranian accounts and track these, in order to effectively assess:
(a) how the Castro regime used the funds deposited in its UBS account through the ECI program;
(b) where are those bills now; and
(c) whether there was any interaction between the Cuban and Iranian accounts.

Should you be unable to provide my colleagues and me with written responses and updates on these inquiries, I request that you make the appropriate officials available to brief us, including in closed session if necessary.

Thank you for your assistance and cooperation.

Sincerely,
Ileana
Ileana Ros-Lehtinen
Member of Congress

cc: The Honorable Henry J. Hyde, Chairman
Committee on International Relations

PRINTED ON RECYCLED PAPER

**U.S. Department of Justice**

*Executive Office for United States Attorneys*
*Office of the Director*

*RFK Main Justice Building, Room 2261*
*950 Pennsylvania Avenue, NW*
*Washington, DC 20530*

*(202) 514-2121*

OCT 18 2004

The Honorable Ileana Ros-Lehtinen
U.S. House of Representatives
Washington, D.C. 20515

Dear Congresswoman Ros-Lehtinen:

This is in response to your letter to United States Attorney David Kelley requesting the status of an investigation of UBS and Cuba.

Because of legal and ethical considerations, we can neither confirm nor deny the existence of particular matters or investigations, nor can we discuss the status of any matter that may be pending in a United States Attorney's Office, other than facts on the public record. Please be assured, however, that the United States Attorney's Office takes all allegations of criminal conduct very seriously and carefully reviews any investigative evidence presented to support such allegations in light of the *Principles of Federal Prosecution.*

We are sorry that we cannot be of further assistance. Please do not hesitate to contact the Department of Justice if we can be of assistance in other matters.

Sincerely,

Mary Beth Buchanan

Mary Beth Buchanan
Director

COMMITTEES:
INTERNATIONAL RELATIONS
GOVERNMENT REFORM
CHAIR:
SUBCOMMITTEE ON MIDDLE EAST AND CENTRAL ASIA
VICE CHAIR:
SUBCOMMITTEE ON WESTERN HEMISPHERE
SUBCOMMITTEE ON WELLNESS AND HUMAN RIGHTS

Congress of the United States
House of Representatives
ILEANA ROS-LEHTINEN
18TH DISTRICT, FLORIDA

PLEASE RESPOND TO:
2160 RAYBURN HOUSE OFFICE BUILDING
WASHINGTON, DC 20515-0918
(202) 225-3931
FAX: (202) 225-5620

DISTRICT OFFICE:
9210 SUNSET DRIVE
SUITE 100
MIAMI, FL 33173
(305) 275-1800
FAX: (305) 275-1801

October 13, 2004

Mr. Marcel Ospel
Chairman
UBS AG
Bahnhofstrasse 45
Zurich, Switzerland 8098

Dear Chairman Ospel:

I am writing to follow-up on inquiries made by colleagues and me during a July 21, 2004 meeting with representatives from the law firm of Sullivan and Cromwell, and an official from the Washington, D.C. office of UBS, regarding UBS transactions under the Extended Custodial Inventory Program with countries subject to U.S. sanctions.

We appreciated their cooperation and thought the meeting was informative and helpful. Nevertheless, it also prompted additional questions regarding transactions with the Cuban regime that remain unanswered. We would appreciate your assistance in facilitating responses to these.

With respect to the transactions with the Cuban regime, the current outstanding issues are:

- Was the account of the Cuban counter-party involved in the transactions with UBS permanently closed? If the account was permanently closed, what happened to the funds in the account?
- During the transactions between UBS and the Cuban counter-party, what was the pattern of activity of the Cuban account? Did the funds remain in the account? Were they transferred to other Swiss banks, other foreign banks? Where are those foreign banks headquartered?
- What economic sectors were the focus of transactions by the Cuban counter-party?
- Was there interaction between the account of the Cuban counter-party and the account of the Iranian counter-party?
- Was there interaction between the account of the Cuban counter-party and U.S. entities?
- What was the annual sum of the transactions between UBS and the Cuban counter-party for the period from 1996 to 2003? Were there any spikes in activity for any particular year?
- Is the Cuban regime or any subunit, affiliated entity, or agent of the regime, still a client of UBS?

We have also previously requested information regarding transactions with the Iranian regime under the ECI program.

I look forward to your response and appreciate your assistance in this matter.

Sincerely,

Ileana Ros-Lehtinen
Member of Congress

COMMITTEES:
INTERNATIONAL RELATIONS
GOVERNMENT REFORM
CHAIR:
SUBCOMMITTEE ON
MIDDLE EAST
AND CENTRAL ASIA
VICE CHAIR:
SUBCOMMITTEE ON
WESTERN HEMISPHERE
SUBCOMMITTEE ON
WELLNESS AND
HUMAN RIGHTS

Congress of the United States
House of Representatives
ILEANA ROS-LEHTINEN
18TH DISTRICT, FLORIDA

PLEASE RESPOND TO:
☐ 2160 RAYBURN HOUSE OFFICE BUILDING
WASHINGTON, DC 20515–0918
(202) 225–3931
FAX: (202) 225–5620

☐ DISTRICT OFFICE:
9210 SUNSET DRIVE
SUITE 100
MIAMI, FL 33173
(305) 275–1800
FAX: (305) 275–1801

September 8, 2004

The Honorable David N. Kelley
United States Attorney
Southern District- New York
One St. Andrews Plaza
New York, New York 10007

Dear Mr. Kelley:

I am writing to ascertain the status of the investigation into the billions of dollars worth of transactions between UBS and the terrorist regime in Cuba, through the Extended Custodial Inventory (ECI) program, in violation of U.S. law.

According to open source reports, your office is looking into a potential nexus out of New York and the potential involvement of U.S. persons in these illegal dealings with countries subject to U.S. sanctions due to their status as state-sponsors of terrorism.

My colleagues and I are exerting oversight over this matter, as part of Congressional activities to address terrorist financing and the policy implications of UBS' actions. Thus, the investigation into this matter of the U.S. Attorney's office for New York's Southern District is of critical importance.

In that vein, my colleagues and I would appreciate receiving an update-- either in the form of a briefing or in writing-- on the status of your investigation, information on the extent and impact of these transactions; and steps that have been or will be undertaken to hold violators accountable for their actions, including the potential for criminal charges to be issued.

I look forward to your response and appreciate your efforts in this regard. Thank you for your assistance and cooperation,

Sincerely,

Ileana Ros-Lehtinen
Member of Congress

cc: The Honorable Henry J. Hyde, Chairman
Committee on International Relations
U.S. House of Representatives

COMMITTEES:
INTERNATIONAL RELATIONS
GOVERNMENT REFORM
CHAIR:
SUBCOMMITTEE ON
MIDDLE EAST
AND CENTRAL ASIA
VICE CHAIR:
SUBCOMMITTEE ON
WESTERN HEMISPHERE
SUBCOMMITTEE ON
WELLNESS AND
HUMAN RIGHTS

Congress of the United States
House of Representatives
ILEANA ROS-LEHTINEN
18TH DISTRICT, FLORIDA

PLEASE RESPOND TO:
2160 RAYBURN HOUSE OFFICE BUILDING
WASHINGTON, DC 20515-0918
(202) 225-3931
FAX: (202) 225-5620

DISTRICT OFFICE:
9210 SUNSET DRIVE
SUITE 100
MIAMI, FL 33173
(305) 275-1800
FAX: (305) 275-1801

August 26, 2004

The Honorable John W. Snow
Secretary
U.S. Department of the Treasury
1500 Pennsylvania Avenue, N.W.
Washington, D.C. 20220

Dear Secretary Snow:

I am writing to follow-up on previous inquiries to you and the Office of Foreign Assets Control, regarding the billions of dollars worth of transactions between UBS and the terrorist regimes in Cuba and Iran, through the Extended Custodial Inventory (ECI) program, in violation of U.S. law.

As indicated in my July 16th letter, my colleagues and I are exerting oversight over this matter, as part of Congressional activities to address terrorist financing and the foreign policy implications of UBS' actions.

The Department of the Treasury's investigation into UBS' conduct to determine possible activities on the part of "US persons" over whom OFAC would have jurisdiction to impose sanctions for potential violations, is of critical importance to our efforts.

In that vein, I would like to formally request a briefing for the week of September 6th to update us on the status of your investigation, detailed information on the extent and impact of these transactions, steps that have been or will be undertaken to hold violators accountable for their actions; and measures implemented to safeguard against such violations and circumventions of U.S. terrorism laws.

I look forward to meeting in September with the appropriate Treasury officials tasked with investigating this matter.

Thank you for your assistance and cooperation,

Sincerely,

Ileana Ros-Lehtinen
Member of Congress

cc: The Honorable Henry J. Hyde
Chairman
Committee on International Relations
U.S. House of Representatives

COMMITTEES:
INTERNATIONAL RELATIONS
GOVERNMENT REFORM

CHAIR:
SUBCOMMITTEE ON
MIDDLE EAST
AND CENTRAL ASIA

VICE CHAIR:
SUBCOMMITTEE ON
WESTERN HEMISPHERE

SUBCOMMITTEE ON
WELLNESS AND
HUMAN RIGHTS

Congress of the United States
House of Representatives
ILEANA ROS-LEHTINEN
18TH DISTRICT, FLORIDA

PLEASE RESPOND TO:
2160 RAYBURN HOUSE OFFICE BUILDING
WASHINGTON, DC 20515-0918
(202) 225-3931
FAX: (202) 225-5620

DISTRICT OFFICE:
9210 SUNSET DRIVE
SUITE 100
MIAMI, FL 33173
(305) 275-1800
FAX: (305) 275-1801

July 16, 2004

The Honorable John W. Snow
Secretary
U.S. Department of the Treasury
1500 Pennsylvania Avenue, N.W.
Washington, D.C. 20220

Dear Secretary Snow:

As you may know, my colleagues and I are looking into the transactions between UBS and terrorist regimes such as Iran, Libya and, in particular, Cuba, through the Extended Custodial Inventory (ECI) program, in violation of U.S. law. Within this context and as part of ongoing Congressional efforts regarding terrorist financing. I would like to formally request a briefing by the Office of Foreign Assets Control on the investigation OFAC has initiated into UBS' conduct to determine possible activities on the part of "U.S. persons" over whom OFAC would have jurisdiction to impose sanctions for potential violations.

Among other issues, we are trying to ascertain: Where did the Cuban regime's funds come from? What was the disposition of the new currency provided by UBS to Cuban counter-parties? How where these funds used? How did UBS and Cuba's terrorist regime use the ECI to facilitate these currency exchanges? Are there any linkages between any "U.S. persons" and these illegal transactions, with UBS, or with the Castro regime and other terrorist states benefiting from these transactions? What was the nature of their involvement?

These are just a few of the questions the Congress must ascertain as part of its oversight efforts. This matter has serious policy implications, particularly with respect to U.S. efforts to deny terrorists and their state-sponsors, such as the Castro regime, the financial resources to pursue their threatening activities.

To that end and, as part of ongoing Congressional efforts on this case, I reiterate the request to receive a briefing by OFAC on its investigation and copies of any relevant materials.

Thank you for your cooperation in this matter.

Sincerely,

Ileana

Ileana Ros-Lehtinen
Member of Congress

COMMITTEES:
INTERNATIONAL RELATIONS
GOVERNMENT REFORM
CHAIR:
SUBCOMMITTEE ON MIDDLE EAST AND CENTRAL ASIA
VICE CHAIR:
SUBCOMMITTEE ON WESTERN HEMISPHERE
SUBCOMMITTEE ON WELLNESS AND HUMAN RIGHTS

Congress of the United States
House of Representatives
ILEANA ROS-LEHTINEN
18TH DISTRICT, FLORIDA

PLEASE RESPOND TO:
2160 RAYBURN HOUSE OFFICE BUILDING
WASHINGTON, DC 20515-0918
(202) 225-3931
FAX: (202) 225-5620

DISTRICT OFFICE:
9210 SUNSET DRIVE
SUITE 100
MIAMI, FL 33173
(305) 275-1800
FAX: (305) 275-1801

July 12, 2004

The Honorable Alan Greenspan
Chairman
Board of Governors of the
Federal Reserve System
20th and Constitution Avenue
Washington, D.C. 20515

Dear Chairman Greenspan:

I appreciate your prompt response to my initial inquiries regarding the transactions between UBS and terrorist regimes such as Iran, Libya and, in particular, Cuba, through the Extended Custodial Inventory (ECI) program, in violation of U.S. law. However, in light of recent information made available to me and within the context of ongoing Congressional efforts regarding terrorist financing, I would like to formally request a copy of the documents/ report relating to the Federal Reserve's investigation referenced in your response of July 9, 2004.

Per your letter, the Federal Reserve investigation revealed that: "UBS's transactions with Cuba through the ECI involved almost exclusively the purchase, by UBS, of about $4 billion of circulated U.S. currency," adding that this currency came "from a single Cuban counterparty." Who is that Cuban entity or agent? Who controlled the accounts? What was the disposition of the funds? How where these funds used? How did UBS and Cuba's terrorist regime manipulate the ECI to facilitate these currency exchanges? Given that UBS knowingly violated U.S. law, can the U.S. trust the value that UBS assigned to the currency obtained from the Castro regime? Are there any linkages between UBS staff involved in these illegal transactions and the Castro regime and other terrorist states benefiting from these transactions?

Given the covert nature of these transactions and the significant amount of money we are dealing with, it is doubtful that these Castro funds derived from tourism but, rather, could have stemmed from one of Castro's nefarious activities, such as drug trafficking.

These are just a few of the questions the Congress must ascertain as part of its oversight efforts. This matter has serious policy implications, particularly with respect to U.S. efforts to deny terrorists and their state-sponsors, such as the Castro regime, the financial resources to pursue their threatening activities.

To that end and, as part of ongoing Congressional efforts on this case, I reiterate the request to receive a copy of the report and other documents relating to the Federal Reserve's investigation, including with a classified annex if necessary.

Thank you for your cooperation in this matter.

Sincerely,

Ileana Ros-Lehtinen
Member of Congress

PRINTED ON RECYCLED PAPER

07/12/04 14:18 FAX 3052751801 ROS-LEHTINEN-DO → DC BACK FAX 001

BOARD OF GOVERNORS
OF THE
FEDERAL RESERVE SYSTEM
WASHINGTON, D. C. 20551

ALAN GREENSPAN
CHAIRMAN

July 9, 2004

The Honorable Ileana Ros-Lehtinen
House of Representatives
Washington D.C. 20515

Dear Congresswoman:

I am writing in response to your recent letter expressing concern over the deceptive conduct of one of the former operators of an Extended Custodial Inventory (ECI) facility, namely UBS AG, a foreign banking organization with principal operations in Switzerland. UBS operated an ECI site in Zurich, Switzerland, on behalf of the Federal Reserve Bank of New York until late October of 2003, when the Reserve Bank terminated its contract with UBS for serious breaches of the contract. In May of 2004, the Federal Reserve assessed a $100 million civil money penalty against UBS for its deceptive conduct both in connection with its performance under the ECI contract, and with respect to the investigation into that performance.

That investigation revealed that UBS violated its ECI Agreement with the Reserve Bank by engaging in U.S. dollar banknote transactions with four countries that were, during the relevant time, subject to sanctions by the U.S. Department of the Treasury's Office of Foreign Assets Control (OFAC): Cuba, Iran, Libya and Yugoslavia. According to the investigative record, unlike its transactions with the other three countries, UBS's transactions with Cuba through the ECI involved almost exclusively the purchase, by UBS, of about $4 billion of circulated U.S. currency. We believe that these funds represented monies spent by tourists in Cuba, and have been informed that the U.S. dollar is the principal currency of the tourist trade in Cuba. The investigation further showed that UBS purchased this currency over an eight-year period from a single Cuban counterparty. UBS did not subcontract with this counterparty. Rather, UBS credited the counterparty's account with UBS in Zurich based on the value that UBS assigned to the purchased currency. It is my understanding that OFAC has initiated an investigation into UBS's conduct to determine whether there were any possible activities on the part of "U.S. persons" over whom OFAC would have jurisdiction to impose sanctions for violations of OFAC rules.

The Honorable Ileana Ros-Lehtinen
Page Two

Please be assured that the prompt corrective action taken to terminate the Federal Reserve's contractual relationship with UBS, and to punish deception by UBS with a large monetary penalty, demonstrates a resolve that Federal Reserve operations will be conducted to the highest standards, and in full compliance with U.S. legal requirements.

Sincerely,

UBS

UBS AG
Financial Services Group
P.O. Box
CH-8098 Zurich
Tel. +41-1-234 11 11

Peter Kurer
Group General Counsel
Member of the Group Executive Board

Bahnhofstrasse 45, 8001 Zürich
Tel. +41-1-234 45 47
Fax +41-1-234 86 55
peter.kurer@ubs.com

www.ubs.com

The Honorable Ileana Ros-Lehtinen
2160 Rayburn House Office Building
U.S. House of Representatives
Washington, D.C. 20515

The Honorable Lincoln Diaz-Balart
2244 Rayburn House Office Building
U.S. House of Representatives
Washington, D.C. 20515

The Honorable Mario Diaz-Balart
313 Cannon House Office Building
U.S. House of Representatives
Washington, D.C. 20515

June 22, 2004

**U.S. Dollar Banknote**

Dear Congresswoman Ros-Lehtinen and Congressmen Diaz-Balart

Our Chairman, Marcel Ospel, has asked me to reply to your letter of June 9, 2004.

Please be assured that both the Board of Directors and the Group Executive Board of UBS share the deep concern expressed in your letter to our Chairman regarding the acts of certain former employees of UBS in their administration of the U.S. dollar banknote Extended Custodial Inventory Program for the Federal Reserve. As you know, the contract with the Federal Reserve relating to the Extended Custodial Inventory Program has been terminated and UBS has exited the bank note trading business for U.S. dollars and other currencies.

As an institution, we profoundly regret, and are deeply embarrassed by, this episode. Please be assured that we are committed to maintaining the highest ethical standards.

Sincerely,

Peter Kurer

cc: Marcel Ospel
Peter Wuffli

**Congress of the United States**
**Washington, DC 20515**
June 9, 2004

Mr. Marcel Ospel
Chairman
UBS AG
Bahnhofstrasse 45
Zurich, Switzerland 8098

Dear Chairman Ospel:

We would like to express our deep concern over the allegations against Switzerland's UBS AG Bank, regarding currency transactions they reportedly conducted through the Extended Custodial Inventory (ECI) program with such terrorist regimes as Iran, Libya, and Cuba. Those states are subject to restrictions from the U.S. Office of Foreign Assets Control (OFAC). We are shocked that a bank entrusted with the crucial responsibility of being an ECI bank, and thus charged with, among other activities, the repatriation of old U.S. currency and the distribution of new U.S. currency, would violate U.S. law the way that UBS AG has been alleged to have done.

Recent news reports have indicated that American armed forces in Iraq discovered $650 million in new United States currency still wrapped in Federal Reserve packaging. Since then, subsequent investigations have found that UBS AG, through their Zurich ECI, conducted ECI transactions, and subsequently falsified documents to cover up the transactions with terrorist states. Approximately $3.9 billion ended up in the hands of the terrorist regime in Havana.

We are greatly disconcerted that UBS AG apparently violated U.S. law for eight years. We hope that further investigations will provide some answers to our many questions concerning this matter. If the allegations are proven to be true, we are disheartened that a company that touts itself as a "premier global asset management business" could be implicated in such a breach of trust.

Sincerely,

Ileana Ros-Lehtinen
Member of Congress

Lincoln Diaz-Balart
Member of Congress

Mario Diaz-Balart
Member of Congress

PRINTED ON RECYCLED PAPER

**Congress of the United States**
**Washington, DC 20515**

June 9, 2004

Chairman Alan Greenspan
Federal Reserve Board
20th and Constitution Avenue
Washington, DC 20515

Dear Chairman Greenspan:

We would like to express our deep concern over the allegations against Switzerland's UBS AG Bank, regarding currency transactions they reportedly conducted through the Extended Custodial Inventory (ECI) program with such terrorist regimes as Iran, Libya, and Cuba. Those states are subject to restrictions from the Office of Foreign Assets Control (OFAC). We are shocked that a bank entrusted with the crucial responsibility of being an ECI bank, and thus charged with, among other activities, the repatriation of old U.S. currency and the distribution of new U.S. currency, would violate U.S. law the way that UBS AG has been alleged to have done.

Recent news reports have indicated that American armed forces in Iraq discovered $650 million in new United States currency still wrapped in Federal Reserve packaging. Since then, subsequent investigations have found that UBS AG, through their Zurich ECI, conducted ECI transactions, and subsequently falsified documents to cover up the transactions with terrorist states. Approximately $3.9 billion ended up in the hands of the terrorist regime in Havana.

We are greatly disconcerted at how UBS AG apparently violated U.S. law for eight years without detection. We request that you investigate exactly what Cuban entities were responsible for changing old U.S. bills, what dealer or bank (subcontracted by UBS) they worked with, and how they were able to circumvent detection. If UBS AG is found guilty of violating United States sanctions, we urge you to investigate further ways (in addition to the $100 million dollar fine that has already been administered) to punish such violations of U.S. law. We look forward to your response to this critical matter.

Sincerely,

Ileana Ros-Lehtinen
Member of Congress

Lincoln Diaz-Balart
Member of Congress

Mario Diaz-Balart
Member of Congress

PRINTED ON RECYCLED PAPER

Ms. ROS-LEHTINEN. Thank you, Mr. Chairman.

If I could just wrap up, I further request that my queries to the Department of Treasury, the Federal Reserve and the U.S. Attorney's office on this matter, along with their responses, also be included in the record.

In closing, I would like to express my appreciation to all of the witnesses appearing before us and I welcome Mr. Rodney Gallagher from the law firm of Gaffney, Gaffney, Gallagher & Philip, which is close to my congressional district in Miami. I have read the testimony provided by all of the witnesses and have specific questions for you if the Chairman permits and, in particular, I would like Mr. Moscow to elaborate on a reference he makes to the system used by the Cuban regime to avoid United States sanctions.

As you know, these are very specific guidelines and restrictions in United States law relating to, for example, agricultural or medical sales to Cuba, and these include prohibitions on any type of export credit or guarantee or any other United States assistance for agricultural sales requiring cash sales only.

I am interested in if the fraudulent scheme can be used to avoid these types of regulations.

Mr. Chairman, I thank you very much for calling this hearing. I look forward to this one and many others that we will have on this very important topic of terrorist financing, offshore banking, corruption, and the war on terror.

Thank you.

Mr. ROHRABACHER. Thank you very much.

Again, with unanimous consent, the questions that you have submitted for the record will be placed into the record and we will be anxious to see the specific answers to those questions.

[The information referred to follows:]

UBS Investment Bank

UBS AG, Stamford Branch
677 Washington Boulevard
Stamford, CT 06901

www.ubs.com

April 21, 2006

The Honorable Dana Rohrabacher
Chairman
House International Relations Subcommittee on Oversight & Investigations
253 Ford House Office Building
Washington, DC 20515

Dear Mr. Chairman:

UBS appreciated the opportunity to appear before your Subcommittee's March 29 hearing entitled, "Offshore Banking, Corruption and the War on Terrorism." Below, as agreed at the hearing, we respond to specific questions raised during the hearing. We also provide additional information relating to UBS' global Sanctions Policy in response to particular comments and questions during the hearing.

For some time now, UBS has maintained stringent anti-money laundering (AML) policies and procedures throughout the world, designed to meet the highest global standards. UBS devotes substantial resources towards preventing money laundering and terror financing, and fully supports law enforcement authorities around the world in these efforts. In addition, UBS is a founding member of the Wolfsberg Group, an association of financial institutions working together to develop state-of-the-art industry standards in the areas of AML and controls to counter terrorist financing.

## I. UBS' Group Global Sanctions Policy

We want to reiterate UBS' strong commitment to money laundering prevention and compliance with the highest global standards. Our global Sanctions Policy underscores our leadership role in fighting money laundering and terrorist financing. We believe our policy is unrivaled by any other international financial institution. At a Senate Banking Committee hearing on April 4, 2006, entitled, "A Current Assessment of Money Laundering and Terrorist Financing Threats and Countermeasures," Treasury Under Secretary for Terrorism and Financial Intelligence Stuart Levey noted:

> We have ample reason to believe that responsible financial institutions around the world pay close attention to such actions and other similar indicators and adjust their business activities accordingly, even if they are not required to do so. A recent example of interest was the announcement by the international bank UBS that it intended to cut off all business with Iran and Syria.

UBS Investment Bank

To date we are not aware of any other non-U.S. bank that has taken such a comprehensive, global approach. While others may now be following our example, we believe we are in the forefront in this area, leading the international financial services industry in its approach to these concerns. As of today, everyone else in the world, except those in the U.S. and UBS, are able to deal with Iran freely.

During the hearing, a number of questions concerned the timing of UBS' decision to adopt its new policy. UBS' senior management decided in January 2005 to cease new business and to exit existing business globally with Cuba and Iran (as well as other sanctioned countries). The firm's senior management directed that a written policy be prepared implementing this decision. UBS' new Sanctions Policy was completed in May 2005, and published on June 16, 2005. As discussed at the hearing, the policy applied voluntary restrictions on the firm's business globally by all parts of the UBS Group with or involving parties in or connected to Cuba, Iran, Myanmar, North Korea, Sudan and Syria. The policy also applied restrictions to dealing with individuals and organizations identified as appearing on various government and other publicly available lists, including, for example, the United Nations Security Council's list of Terrorists and Supporters of Terrorism, as well as the European Union's list, the Swiss State Secretariat for Economic Affairs' list, and the U.S. Treasury Department's Office of Foreign Asset Control list of Specially Designated Nationals and Blocked Persons. These voluntary restrictions are above and beyond the strict requirement to comply with the national laws and regulations prevailing in any specific jurisdiction.

Following the adoption of this policy, all business lines were directed to review their businesses and activities and to establish implementation plans and controls. These reviews and plans progressed, culminating in the agreement by November 2005 on specific plans and processes to complete the full implementation of the new policy.

During the hearing, questions were raised about specific aspects of UBS' policy. To be clear, the following statements accurately describe UBS' policy:

- UBS' Sanctions Policy aggregates all the U.S., United Nations, Swiss and European Union sanctions restrictions as well as additional UBS-imposed requirements. Under UBS' policy, it is not a matter of complying with only one of the above requirements; it is a matter of complying with all of them.

- UBS never has had, and does not have today, any accounts for Fidel Castro. On the basis of our global policy, UBS would not today open an account for or offer services to Fidel Castro or any other member of the Cuban regime (or indeed any other sanctioned country's regime).

UBS Investment Bank

**II. Specific Questions**

1. How many individuals were terminated for their conduct in operating the ECI program?

In total, eight individuals who had some involvement in either the operation of, or the investigation into, the ECI Program left UBS directly or indirectly as a result of such involvement.

- Four employees (two Executive Directors, one Director and one Associate Director) directly concerned with operating the ECI facility were dismissed summarily.
- The most senior manager (a Managing Director), with overall responsibility for (but no operational involvement in) the ECI facility was terminated.
- Three senior members of the Legal, Compliance and Risk functions (two Managing Directors and one Executive Director) were given formal written or oral warnings and/or suffered bonus reductions and in each case left UBS voluntarily.

2. Does UBS hold accounts for Slobodan Milosevic?

UBS does not now hold, nor has it ever held, an account for Slobodan Milosevic.

3. Does UBS hold accounts for Saddam Hussein?

UBS does not now hold, nor has it ever held, an account for Saddam Hussein.

4. Does UBS hold accounts for Osama bin Laden?

UBS does not now hold, nor has it ever held, an account for Osama bin Laden.

As has previously been stated publicly, UBS did maintain a relationship between 1990 and 1991 with members of the bin Laden family, which, as you know, is a large, well-known family with global business interests. Osama bin Laden never received any asset distribution when the assets were distributed among his family members in 1991; none of the family members receiving distributions appear on any U.S. sanctions lists. As you're aware, he was disowned by his family.

UBS originally provided information about this closed account to the Swiss Money Laundering Reporting Office in 2001 which forwarded it to the Swiss Federal Deputy Attorney General. After that, it was made available to the U.S. authorities.

5. Was the account of the Cuban counterparty involved in the ECI transactions with UBS permanently closed? If so, where are the funds that were in the account?

UBS Investment Bank

The Cuban counterparty's account was closed during 2005 as part of the implementation of UBS' new Sanctions Policy. On closure, the balance remaining in the account was transferred to an account held by the Cuban counterparty with an unaffiliated bank incorporated within the European Union.

6. Did the funds remain at UBS or were they transferred to other banks? Were these foreign banks and, if so, where are they headquartered?

As noted above, the Cuban counterparty's funds are no longer with UBS. The final balances were transferred to an account held by the Cuban counterparty with an unaffiliated bank incorporated within the European Union.

7. What was the pattern of activity in the account? Were there any spikes in activity and for what purpose?

UBS' review of certain transactions with the Cuban counterparty has not identified any transactions raising suspicions of money laundering. As part of our review, we compared transactions from this account against the profile of activity one would expect to see for this type of customer and found them to be consistent.

The specific activity as reviewed consisted primarily of purchases by UBS of USD banknotes from the Cuban counterparty. These purchases took place over the seven year period 1996 to 2003. Although volumes broadly increased year-on-year during the period, there were no evident spikes in activity that were inconsistent with our understanding of the source of funds.

UBS believes that the banknotes it purchased from the Cuban bank were derived from legitimate activities -- tourism and remittances to family members made by Cuban émigrés. U.S. banknotes attributable to tourism activity in Cuba and remittances to Cuba also increased over the given period and at the relevant times we believe substantially exceeded the level of banknotes sold by the Cuban bank to UBS.

In exchange for the purchases of USD banknotes, UBS credited the Cuban bank's account. Generally, the credits on the Cuban counterparty's account did not remain with UBS. The transactions we reviewed showed that a majority of the funds were transferred to accounts that the Cuban counterparty held with other international banks, including banks in Asia and Europe.

8. Was there any interaction between the Cuban and Iranian counterparties?

UBS has seen no evidence to suggest that the ECI program was used to facilitate interaction between the Cuban and the Iranian financial institutions that engaged in banknote transactions with UBS.

UBS Investment Bank

Thank you again for providing UBS the opportunity to participate in last month's hearing and to provide you with additional information. We trust that our responses satisfy the outstanding questions raised at the hearing.

Sincerely,

Michael E. Herde

UBS AG

cc: The Honorable William Delahunt
The Honorable Ileana Ros-Lehtinen
The Honorable Ed Royce
The Honorable Joe Wilson

Mr. ROHRABACHER. Mr. Wilson, do you have an opening statement?

Mr. WILSON. Mr. Chairman, I do not. I just want to thank you for getting the hearing together and I appreciate the persons being here today, but I particularly appreciate your leadership and I am delighted to be here.

Mr. ROHRABACHER. All right. We thank you very much.

On hearing Ms. Ros-Lehtinen's description of breaking the wall down and finding this treasure house of cash, it is maybe symbolic of what we are trying to do at this hearing today, to break down the wall and find out what is going on behind that wall and where that money has come from and where it is going to. The public deserves to know.

Our first panel, we will hear from Assistant District Attorney Arthur Middlemiss, who is the Bureau Chief of the Investigations Division Central, a part of the Investigations Division of the New York County District Attorney's Office that is responsible for investigating and prosecuting banking and security frauds. He was named to this post December 2004. He has supervised many significant investigations, including the 2005 investigation into the Israeli Discount Bank of New York. In 2003, he co-led the District Attorney's 18-month investigation into the role of New York-based financial institutions in the Enron collapse.

We thank you very much.

Next, we will hear from, in the first panel, Mr. Michael Herde, who is the Managing Director of UBS's Investment Bank Region Americas as Head of Compliance. Mr. Herde will discuss the role of UBS and the bank's operation of the Extended Custodial Inventory program as it relates to Cuba and Iran.

We thank you, Mr. Herde, for being with us. We thank the bank for what I consider to be a demonstration of good faith that you are sitting there, willing to participate in this hearing, and so we appreciate you and your bank's representation.

So with that said, I usually admonish witnesses to keep their testimony down to 5 minutes, but I do not see how we can do that in this particular case. I would think that a number of issues have been brought up that you might want to comment on and so please do not take a half an hour, but if you could make sure you have laid the foundation for the discussion that will follow.

Thank you very much.

Mr. Middlemiss, you may begin.

## STATEMENT OF ARTHUR D. MIDDLEMISS, ESQ., ASSISTANT DISTRICT ATTORNEY, BUREAU CHIEF, INVESTIGATIONS DIVISION CENTRAL, NEW YORK COUNTY DISTRICT ATTORNEY'S OFFICE

Mr. MIDDLEMISS. Thank you, Mr. Chairman. I will be relatively brief in my remarks and be happy to answer whatever questions the Subcommittee has about the cases that have been prosecuted by the Manhattan D.A.'s office.

Let me thank you, Mr. Chairman and Members of the Subcommittee, for inviting me to speak today as part of this important panel.

Mr. Chairman, as you noted, I am an Assistant District Attorney in Manhattan and to clear up whatever error occurred in the typo, I am most decidedly a local prosecutor, albeit one who works for district attorney with an international reputation, that being Robert M. Morgenthau, who has served as the New York County District Attorney since 1975.

It is perhaps a combination of the location of the New York County D.A.'s office and the interest and sophistication of Mr. Morgenthau in prosecuting these crimes that leads a representative of his office to be sitting before you today.

The simple fact is that sophisticated crimes often involve international money flows and many of the cases that I have summarized in my remarks bear that out.

In 2004, Mr. Morgenthau appointed me to run a bureau in the D.A.'s office called Investigations Division Central (IDC). That bureau had formerly been run by another of your panelists here today, Mr. John Moscow, who preceded me in the position.

As summarized in my written remarks, IDC, the bureau that I run in the office, has prosecuted several cases involving the international money remittance business. For example, Beacon Hill was an unlicensed money remitter that moved $6.5 billion in 6 years from South America through New York. More recently, we investigated a case involving the Israel Discount Bank of New York that enabled illegal Brazilian businesses to move another $2.2 billion through New York. In the last year, we have also successfully prosecuted three illegal money remitters in New York who moved $132 million from New York to Vietnam.

Mr. ROHRABACHER. Before you go on, could you tell us what you mean by moved through?

Mr. MIDDLEMISS. Certainly, Mr. Chairman. With respect to the money remitters themselves, these businesses were essentially in the business of collecting money from people who wanted to send it abroad and made that happen, very similar to the way that a Western Union would operate, except without any of the safeguards that are built in with a Western Union type transaction. For example, one of the money remitters that we prosecuted in New York essentially would take clients' money in several times, in fact, hundreds of times, more than $10,000 at a clip. Instead of filing any CTRs (Currency Transaction Report), none were filed, none of the activity was scrutinized for suspicious activity, so no suspicious activity reports were filed, and none of the identities of the persons who were transmitting these huge sums of money to Vietnam were screened through the OFAC (Office of Foreign Assets Control) process to see if they were known terrorists, drug traffickers, or other criminals on that list.

Mr. ROHRABACHER. Excuse me for taking the prerogative, but why did they not just send it to Vietnam in the first place? Why did they have to go through somebody in New York?

Mr. MIDDLEMISS. Well, probably one of the reasons is that they wanted to avoid any regulatory scrutiny whatsoever. What they paid for, the service that they got from the illegal business that we prosecuted, was secrecy, essentially. They did not have to open a bank account in their name. They did not have to submit themselves to whatever scrutiny that bank would have. There were no reporting requirements to the U.S. Government. In short, if you wanted to move money illegally from New York to Vietnam, these three businesses provided you an excellent means to do that.

Mr. ROHRABACHER. You said they went to Brazil to New York to Vietnam?

Mr. MIDDLEMISS. Yes.

Mr. ROHRABACHER. Why did the Brazilians go through New York rather than just go directly to Vietnam?

Mr. MIDDLEMISS. I think that we have had some miscommunication. Several of the cases that we have prosecuted have involved huge sums of money coming from Brazil through New York. A separate set of cases that the office has prosecuted have dealt with businesses in New York that have moved money to Vietnam. The businesses are similar in that they offer the clientele the benefit of secrecy, no SAR (Suspicious Activity Report) filings, no CTRs, no OFAC screening, but there are two separate types of businesses that we have prosecuted.

Mr. ROHRABACHER. I still do not understand why they would go through New York. Pardon me for getting stuck on this, but why would someone in Brazil—it is one thing, we understand people carrying brown paper bags across the border or something, but why would someone in Brazil want to go through New York and then have it transferred rather than just going straight to Vietnam?

Mr. MIDDLEMISS. Let me step back and perhaps answer the question this way. For Brazilians, there are essentially two ways for them to get money out of Brazil and, not to make this simplistic, but there is a legal way and an illegal way.

The legal way requires Brazilians to register their outgoing money transfers with the Brazilian Central Bank. That exposes them to Brazilian regulatory scrutiny. For example, they know how much money you have if you register that it is going out of the country.

If you do it the illegal way, you use what in Portuguese is called a "doleiro" or a "casa de cambio," which essentially is a money exchanger in Brazil and these companies in Brazil are—what they can do is change money for you, like a money exchanger here. What they cannot do legally is to send money out of the country. Despite this, on a regular basis, these doleiros have managed to open up accounts with United States financial institutions, whereby they accept money on behalf of their Brazilian clientele and then wire it to their account at the New York bank. This enables the Brazilian citizen or Brazilian criminal, because we really do not know, to have access to the United States financial system and people in Brazil want to get their money out for currency stability, because they want access to the efficiencies that are provided by our financial system, and from New York, once it gets here and you are engaging in a dollar transaction, you can move your money to the Caribbean or another offshore location and you can take advantage of all the benefits of secrecy of tax havens or offshore financial centers.

For example, a Brazilian wants to send $100 million out of Brazil. He takes it to a doleiro in Brazil. The Brazilian doleiro has an account with, for example, Israel Discount Bank in New York. The transaction from the Brazilian standpoint will look like the

Brazilian doleiro sending $100 million to the bank in New York. Once it gets to the bank in New York, the customer in Brazil can instruct the doleiro to move that money from New York, essentially wherever he wants it to go, including an account that that individual himself has opened up at IDB.

These are some of the advantages that you have if you are a Brazilian citizen.

Now, what this exposes us to in the United States is the fact that the bank's client, to wit, the doleiro, has clients of its own, and the doleiro does not scrutinize the activity of its clients for suspicious activity. So this exposes us to scenarios that we have seen where, for example, huge sums of money are coming out of parts of Brazil through doleiros that simply do not have the industrial base to send those sums of money, and we can draw certain inferences about the source of that money from that fact.

We have worked closely with Brazilian prosecutors in the Manhattan D.A.'s office. We know for a fact that one individual, the former Governor and Mayor of the city and state of Sao Paolo in Brazil, an individual named Paolo Maluf, moved as much as $250 million that was the proceeds of a kickback scheme in Sao Paolo through doleiros to New York and on to what are considered offshore financial centers.

Mr. Maluf is presently under indictment in Brazil for essentially having stolen this money and illegally moved it out of Brazil.

The fact that he was able to do it through New York leads me to one of the points that I wanted to make before the Subcommittee. With IDB, for example, IDB's clients were engaged in illegal activity.

Mr. DELAHUNT. Can you tell us who IDB is?

Mr. MIDDLEMISS. I am sorry, sir. That is an acronym for Israel Discount Bank of New York. As summarized in our remarks, we did an investigation in conjunction with the New York State Banking Department and the FDIC (Federal Deposit Insurance Corporation) that led to a settlement with IDB (Israel Discount Bank) based on deficiencies that IDB had in its anti-money laundering policies.

IDB, as a result of this settlement with the Manhattan D.A., with the FDIC, with New York State Banking, essentially had to put in a regimen of hopefully better anti-money laundering controls, as well as pay a fine of $8.5 million to the city and state of New York and I believe as much as $16.5 million additional civil money penalties to FINCEN (Financial Crimes Enforcement Network), the FDIC and other Federal regulators, as well as the New York State Banking Department.

Mr. DELAHUNT. How much was it?

Mr. MIDDLEMISS. $8.5 million as a fine to the city and state of New York, and as much as $16.5 million in civil money penalties to the other agencies involved in the settlement.

Mr. ROHRABACHER. You may proceed with your testimony.

Mr. MIDDLEMISS. I think the point that I was trying to make was that the individuals at Israel Discount Bank essentially had clients who were engaged in illegal activity.

Now, we look upon our banks as having to know their customers and put teeth into the compliance regimen. I think it is interesting to look at the New York bank's activities from the perspective of the Brazilian prosecutors.

The Brazilian prosecutor is faced with a bank in another jurisdiction that enables criminals and others to move massive amounts of money out of his country. The evidence of those transactions is located in New York, far away from Brazil and difficult for the Brazilian prosecutor to obtain. The money is also located in New York, and it is hard for a Brazilian prosecutor to forfeit that money, should he identify a bad guy in Brazil that he is prosecuting.

From the perspective of the Brazilian prosecutor, our bank was the offshore bank and I am sure that they had the same complaints about our banks that will be voiced during this hearing and I am sure others regarding offshore financial centers.

So in sum, my remarks come down to we should basically exercise the Golden Rule and that what is good for the goose is good for the gander. If we want to control illegal monies going to offshore jurisdictions, we should look at and force our banks to live up to the substance of the rules, the compliance rules, that Congress has written for them to do. If they do not, then a lot of the exercise that we go through in trying to track down money and to prosecute these crimes essentially will be fruitless. And I also think that it would be more of an incentive to encourage other jurisdictions to put in place anti-money laundering controls if our banks themselves are willing to live up to our own.

[The prepared statement of Mr. Middlemiss follows:]

PREPARED STATEMENT OF ARTHUR D. MIDDLEMISS, ESQ., ASSISTANT DISTRICT ATTORNEY, BUREAU CHIEF, INVESTIGATIONS DIVISION CENTRAL, NEW YORK COUNTY DISTRICT ATTORNEY'S OFFICE

Thank you, Mr. Chairman and members of the Subcommittee, for inviting me to speak today. My name is Arthur Middlemiss. I'm an assistant district attorney in Manhattan, and I work for Robert M. Morgenthau. Since late 2004, I have run a bureau at the Manhattan D.A.'s Office called Investigation Division Central, or IDC.

IDC, as does other office bureaus, prosecutes banking and securities frauds, many of them having international ramifications. Manhattan, a world center for banking and securities transactions, is home to many financial institutions, which sophisticated criminals use to defraud investors, companies, and even foreign governments of billions of dollars. Even in cases of domestic fraud, criminals often conduct some of their activities outside the United States, keeping funds and incriminating evidence overseas away from police and prosecutors. IDC works with foreign governments, victims, and multi-national corporations to conduct extensive international investigations so that it can uncover and prosecute large-scale frauds and thefts. Through IDC's efforts, more than one billion dollars has been returned to investors, and hundreds of defendants have been convicted and sentenced.

My comments today will focus in two areas: 1) the international money remittance business, and 2) the role offshore jurisdictions play in securities fraud cases here in the United States. I hope to explain some of the concerns that regulators and law enforcement have about some practices among banks and businesses in the money service industry, and to express Mr. Morgenthau's hope to encourage legitimate businesses, banks, and other financial institutions to take appropriate action when they see the red flags that should alert them to illegal activities.

MONEY TRANSMISSION AND MONEY LAUNDERING

The best way for me to give you some idea of the dimensions of the problems we are facing in regards to money laundering and the urgent need to do something about them, is to describe some of the cases involving money service businesses we have prosecuted at the Manhattan District Attorney's Office.

Over the past several years, the Manhattan District Attorney's Office has focused on underground remittance systems and the financial institutions that allow them to operate. To be sure, legitimate money service businesses play an important role in the lives of many New Yorkers, especially for recent immigrants, many of whom rely on check cashers to cash their checks, and on money remitters to send money home to their families. However, unlicensed, and therefore unregulated, money service businesses pose to a threat to the integrity of the nation's financial system and to our safety and well-being.

As Mr. Morgenthau has said, "These underground remittance systems provide a window of opportunity for many types of criminals to move their ill-gotten gains: narcotics traffickers, gun smugglers, corrupt foreign politicians, and terrorists." To date, the Manhattan District Attorney's Office has prosecuted a number of these financial businesses, which together have wired more than $9.8 billion worldwide.

The businesses prosecuted by the Manhattan District Attorney were—like all money service businesses—obligated under both federal and state law to develop and implement effective anti-money laundering programs, to file suspicious activity reports ("SARs") with law enforcement if suspicious activity was identified, to follow currency transaction reporting ("CTR") requirements for transactions over $10,000, and to screen customers' identification against lists of known terrorists and narcotics traffickers ("OFAC"). In the face of those regulations, the subjects of the Manhattan District Attorney's investigation enabled their customers to avoid all regulatory scrutiny and to move massive amounts of money worldwide anonymously.

For example, in February 2004, with the assistance of the New York State Banking Department, Beacon Hill Services Corporation ("Beacon Hill") was convicted, after a jury trial, for operating as an unlicensed money transmitter; in its last six years of operation, Beacon Hill had moved more than $6.5 billion through accounts it maintained at a major New York bank.

Beacon Hill was operating as a money transmitter without a license, a felony under New York State law. Beacon Hill ran its money transmitting business out of offices on the seventh floor of a midtown Manhattan office building. It had about a dozen employees. It was open for business from 1994 to February 2003, when we executed a search warrant on the premises.

It is doubtful that very much of this money was moved through Beacon Hill for legitimate purposes. Legitimate clients would have dealt directly with a bank rather than pay the extra fees required to do business through Beacon Hill. What the clients got for their extra money was secrecy and protection from the scrutiny of government authorities. Beacon Hill did not keep proper records and much of its business was transacted with offshore shell corporations and "casas de cambio," or exchange houses, in Brazil and Uruguay. Accordingly, it was nearly impossible to identify the real parties in interest behind Beacon Hill's transactions, or to trace the money through the company's accounts. Nonetheless, it is reasonable to believe that a great portion of the money that passed through Beacon Hill's accounts was linked to unlawful capital flight, narcotics trafficking or other criminal activities. We do not know the extent to which the facilities of Beacon Hill may have been used to fund terrorist activities. Records do show, however, that Beacon Hill transmitted $31.5 million to accounts in Pakistan, Lebanon, Jordan, Dubai, Saudi Arabia, and elsewhere in the Middle East.

After the Manhattan District Attorney indicted Beacon Hill, we met with Brazilian police officials and prosecutors and representatives of a special commission investigating the movement of some $30 billion out of Brazil. Much of this was thought to be the proceeds of official corruption, government fraud, organized crime activities, and weapons and narcotics trafficking. More than $200 million of this money had moved through Beacon Hill and accounts at other New York banks; these funds were alleged to have belonged to Paulo Maluf, the former mayor and governor of the city and state of San Paolo, Brazil. Maluf now faces charges in Brazil that he stole hundreds of million of dollars as part of a construction kickback scheme.

The above-described meeting was not the only example of cooperation between Brazilian and New York authorities. In August 2004, Brazilian law enforcement authorities, in the largest operation of its kind, executed over 120 search warrants and over sixty arrest warrants, and charged over 100 individuals with money laundering and related financial crimes throughout Brazil as part of Operation "Farol da Colina"—Portuguese for "Beacon Hill." This operation was based in part on information gathered from the Manhattan District Attorney's investigation and prosecution of Beacon Hill. Close cooperation between the Manhattan District Attorney's Office and Brazilian federal police and prosecutors continues.

The Manhattan District Attorney has also focused on the role played by the United States banks and financial institutions that allow these illegal activities to go on. As the District Attorney has said, he will not "tolerate violations of the requirements that [U.S. financial institutions] know their customers and adhere to all anti-money laundering standards. Financial institutions that harbor illegal operations will be investigated and appropriate steps will be taken to ensure their compliance with the law."

For example, Beacon Hill itself conducted its business through accounts maintained, for nine years, at a major New York bank. This illegal business was able to flourish for as long as it did only because the bank closed its eyes to numerous warning signs that the accounts posed a high risk for money laundering.

There were several red flags raised by Beacon Hill's business that the bank involved should have recognized. First, many of Beacon Hill's clients were themselves in the business of moving money to South America, and the identities of their customers were unknown and unknowable by the bank. Wire transfer documents often identified the beneficiaries of transfers only as a "customer" or "valued customer." Other Beacon Hill clients were offshore shell corporations. A large portion of Beacon Hill's business was run out of a pooled account which served many customers, making it impossible to link deposits with transfers out of the account. Finally, the London office of the bank had shut down Beacon Hill's accounts in 1994 and, as the bank knew, Beacon Hill did not have a license to operate in the State of New York. As Mr. Morgenthau has stated, "It is fair to say that, in this case, the bank's compliance department completely fell down on the job."

As a result of leads developed during the Beacon Hill investigation, the District Attorney's Office launched an investigation into Hudson United Bank ("HUB"). On March 2, 2004, the District Attorney's Office reached a settlement with HUB relating to the failure of the HUB branch located at 90 Broad Street in Manhattan to monitor and assess accurately the money-laundering risks posed by its international wire transfer business. Specifically, the HUB accounts engaged in more than $65 million of transactions originating or terminating with individuals and companies doing business in the tri-border region of South America (formed by the borders of Paraguay, Argentina and Brazil), as well as with other bogus South American money transmitters. As part of the settlement, HUB agreed to reform its anti-money laundering policies and procedures, and to pay a total of $5 million to the City of New York, which included costs of the investigation.

During the course of both the Beacon Hill and HUB investigations, the District Attorney's Office developed leads indicating that Israel Discount Bank of New York ("IDBNY") accounts were also being used to facilitate and conduct illegal money transfers from Brazil. The investigation into those leads disclosed that IDBNY's private banking customers, both individuals and companies, would bring Brazilian currency to "doleiros" (foreign exchange houses) in Brazil. These doleiros are authorized to conduct currency exchanges in Brazil, but are not authorized to engage in foreign money transfers. The doleiros would then transfer money from the doleiro accounts at IDBNY to the private banking client's account at IDBNY. The funds would then go wherever IDBNY was instructed to send them. This process evaded Brazil's strict controls over foreign money transfers and was illegal in Brazil. Thus, in reality, the doleiros were conducting money transfer businesses in New York, through their operations in their IDBNY account.

In addition to breaking Brazilian law, this particular "nesting" violated United States and New York banking regulations and money laundering laws. IDBNY failed to maintain accurate and complete customer information in violation of state and federal rules. IDBNY's money-laundering policies, systems and controls failed to prevent illegal transfers from passing through accounts at IDBNY. IDBNY also violated regulations governing the filing of SARs by failing to report suspicious transactions in a timely manner and in an accurate and complete manner.

In a related operation, authorities in New York and Brazil took action against Transmar Turismo ("Transmar"), an illegal money transmitter with offices in Brazil, who had used its account at IDBNY to make illegal money transfers. While Manhattan prosecutors froze Transmar's account at IDBNY in Manhattan, the Brazilian federal police executed seven search warrants on the offices of Transmar, as well as at the offices and homes of its principal owners and officers. The president of the company, Algemiro Moutinho, was taken into custody pursuant to an arrest warrant issued by a Brazilian federal judge. Moutinho and two other officers of Transmar were charged with Money Laundering, Crimes Against the National Financial System (operating an illegal money remittance business), Managing a Financial Institution with Fraud, and Racketeering. Meanwhile, prosecutors in Manhattan will seek to forfeit the assets in Transmar's New York accounts.

In short, the District Attorney's investigation revealed that IDBNY had deficiencies in its anti-money laundering policies and controls. As a result of those deficiencies, IDBNY failed to monitor the risks that its customers were engaged in illegal activity, and enabled certain bank customers to move over $2.2 billion illegally from Brazil into IDBNY.

Along with the New York State Banking Department and the Federal Deposit Insurance Corporation ("FDIC"), the District Attorney's Office entered a settlement with IDBNY that required IDBNY to install a regimen of compliance and controls to insure that the bank complies with all anti-money laundering requirements. In addition, IDBNY was required to pay $8.5 million to the City and State of New York, and to cover the costs of the investigation. IDBNY may face additional Civil Money Penalties not to exceed $16.5 million in the aggregate to NYSBD, the FDIC, and the United States Department of the Treasury's Financial Crimes Enforcement Network ("FinCen").

With the participation of the New York State Banking Department, the Manhattan District Attorney's Office has also prosecuted other illegal, unlicensed money service businesses operating out of Manhattan, some literally within a stone's throw of our Office. Three of these businesses successfully enabled their customers to move more than $132 million anonymously over the last five years to Vietnam. For the most part, the operators of these businesses simply used their bank accounts to conduct their transactions. They would take their customers' money, bundle it together, deposit it into bank accounts, and send it abroad, where it was separated and distributed according to the customers' instructions.

To their credit, some banks recognized that these businesses were unlicensed, and therefore illegal, and refused to do business with them. However, at least three New York banks allowed these illegal businesses to operate using bank facilities, even though the highly questionable nature of their activities should have been obvious to the banks. Of course, had the banks truly known their customer, and thus been positioned to assess whether their customer's activity was suspicious or not, they would have known that these businesses did not have licenses to transmit money, and thus were operating illegally.

In the case of these three businesses, some of the money involved was likely sent home by immigrants to support their families. We know that because some of the amounts were small, a couple of hundred of dollars. Other transactions, however, involved large sums of cash. Because these businesses were unlicensed, they did not file CTRs or SARs, and did not make and keep the records they were obligated to about their customers' activities; for that reason it is nearly impossible to sort out the legitimate transfers from the illegitimate. What we do know, however, is that if someone wanted to move a lot of money out of New York without garnering regulatory or law enforcement scrutiny—and plenty of criminals want to do just that—these illegal businesses provided an open window through which to do it.

Money laundering poses a real threat to our collective well-being because it facilitates a wide range of criminal activities, from tax evasion to international terrorism. Like other criminal organizations, international terrorist networks need money to function. Terrorist networks need funds for training and supplies and to support their operatives around the world; they also need to able to receive and transmit funds across national borders, including our own. In investigations at the Manhattan District Attorney's Office, we have seen tens of millions of dollars transmitted to and from parties in the tri-border region of Brazil, Argentina and Paraguay, which is notorious for supplying funds to terrorist groups in the Middle East.

## OFFSHORE JURISDICTIONS AND SECURITIES FRAUD

I also want to comment on the role that offshore jurisdictions play in securities fraud cases here in the Untied States. Many of the New York-crimes investigated by IDC involve "offshore jurisdictions," tax havens such as the Cayman Islands, the Bahamas, and the British Virgin Islands, which have no significant economies of their own, but use their strict bank and corporate secrecy laws to attract money from more developed countries. Because of their unwillingness to share information with lawful authorities from other countries, these jurisdictions present extraordinary difficulties for regulators and law enforcement authorities in the United States and other developed countries. For the same reason, they present opportunities to criminals.

Companies and accounts in the tax haven countries often play an integral role in a securities fraud scheme. For example, the Manhattan District Attorney's Office has convicted four New York stockbrokers of using MasterCards issued on offshore bank accounts to launder more than $750,000 realized from fraudulent stock deals. The proceeds from the stock fraud were paid to the brokers into accounts at the Leadenhall Bank & Trust in Nassau, the Bahamas. The brokers, who have since been convicted of felonies and barred from the securities industry, withdrew more than $750,000, using MasterCards at ATM machines in New York City and Atlantic City, New Jersey, among other places.

Notably, it is not only stock fraudsters that use offshore debit cards for illegal ends. In July 2004, we convicted a doctor for evading taxes on $300,000 of income, $126,000 of which he put into an account at Leadenhall in the form of checks, ostensibly in payment of rent for his office. In fact, he owned the building in which he had the office. Like the crooked brokers, the doctor used a MasterCard to withdraw money at ATMs and to make purchases with the offshore funds. The doctor also used offshore accounts and a shell company to shelter another $76,000 of income that he failed to report.

In another case, a real estate agent used an account at Leadenhall to hide income of approximately $75,000 from her real estate business that was earned in New York. The real estate agent sent the money to the Bahamas by use of Fed Ex packages, the charges for which appeared on her American Express card. The defendant accessed the offshore account from the United States by use of a debit card that she used to make purchases in Manhattan and elsewhere.

As part of the offshore credit card investigation, which was conducted with the assistance of the New York State Department of Taxation and Finance, we learned that, in 2001, 115,000 separate offshore MasterCard accounts were used in the New York, New Jersey, and Connecticut area. The MasterCards were used in 2001 to access over $100 million that had been deposited in banks located in at least seventeen secrecy jurisdictions, including the Bahamas, Barbados, Belize, and the Cayman Islands.

The same offshore tools available to the above-referenced stockbrokers, doctor and real estate agent to commit relatively simple securities crimes and to evade taxes are also used to conduct more sophisticated schemes. For example, in a 2003 case, a solicitor from London, England, Andrew Warren, pled guilty to Attempted Enterprise Corruption, a class "C" New York felony, in connection with a stock fraud conspiracy operating in Great Britain and New York.

The criminal enterprise was run by principals of Westfield Financial Corporation, a broker-dealer on Park Avenue, in Manhattan. In the scheme, securities were sold pursuant to SEC Regulation S—which permits the sale of unregistered securities to foreign investors—to some twenty companies chartered in Liberia and the British Virgin Islands, and ostensibly managed from the Isle of Jersey, one of the Channel Islands. In fact, the offshore companies were merely nominees for insiders from the New York metropolitan area, who bought the Reg S stock on margin, ran up the price in trading between the Jersey companies, and used the stock they bought on the cheap to cover their own short sales, cashing in for millions at the expense of innocent investors and the companies that issued the stock.

In November 2002, two other lawyers were convicted on charges of participating in a related scheme. The defendants in that case, Stuart Creggy and Harry J.F. Bloomfield, were convicted of conspiracy and falsifying business records after a six-week trial.

Creggy was a senior partner at the law firm of Talbot Creggy in London. He was also a part-time Magistrate Judge for Westminster and Kensington, in London. Bloomfield had been a lawyer in Montreal, Canada, a senior partner in the Bloomfield, Bellemare law firm, a Queen's Counsel, and an honorary counsel for the country of Liberia. Creggy and Bloomfield recruited others, including Liberian diplomats, to pretend to be the owners of the off-shore companies. The off-shore companies, established in Liberia and the British Virgin Islands, among other places, were used by the defendants' clients for various purposes, including the Regulation S scheme that was the subject of Warren's guilty plea.

Another securities-related matter involved an offshore investment fund known as Evergreen Security, Ltd., which was chartered in the British Virgin Islands and had offices in the Bahamas. Investors in Evergreen, which was actually managed from offices in Orlando, Florida, were promised an annual return of 9% to 10% on funds nominally held in offshore trusts organized in the Bahamas and Costa Rica. In fact, Evergreen was run as a Ponzi scheme, with the money from later investors being used to pay earlier investors. Thousands of Evergreen investors were defrauded. No doubt, it was the allure of investments in lucrative offshore trusts, marketed to the public as "asset protection trusts," that attracted so much money to Evergreen in the first place. Investors lost $330 million in fraud; Evergreen filed for bankruptcy in January 2001.

Five defendants were convicted in New York in connection with the thefts from the Evergreen fund totaling over $34.2 million. In each of the thefts, money was transferred from Evergreen to offshore shell companies controlled by one or more of the defendants. Other defendants, including one of those convicted in New York, were convicted in federal court in Tampa, Florida.

Offshore entities also played a central role in facilitating the notorious accounting fraud at Enron Corporation. In July 2003, the Manhattan District Attorney's Office, along with the SEC, announced a settlement with J.P. Morgan Chase and Citigroup, concluding an eighteen-month investigation into $8.3 billion in loans that had been structured by the banks in such as way that permitted Enron to account falsely for the transactions in its financial statements.

Our investigation showed that the loans to Enron were structured as prepaid forward commodities transactions between the banks, Enron, and ostensibly independent counterparties offshore. In fact, the offshore parties were so-called "Special Purpose Entities" located in the Isle of Jersey and the Caymans which the banks controlled and which were involved in the deals only to make them look like commodities trades; this was done to accommodate Enron's desire to be able to account for the revenue as cash flows from operations rather than cash from bank financings. These sham transactions contributed to Enron's collapse, which had disastrous effects for thousands of Enron's employees and shareholders.

---

As Mr. Morgenthau points out in his public remarks, which themselves are the source of the vast majority of information provided herein, there are international aspects to many, if not most, sophisticated frauds. In today's global economy, it is increasingly rare to encounter a significant financial crime that is strictly a local matter. Prosecutors pursue these cases to extent we can, but criminal investigations and prosecutions are far from a complete answer to the problem.

Law enforcement cannot do the job of policing illegal money flows alone. We need the cooperation of the money service and banking industries to know who they are dealing with and to help identify other businesses that may be operating illegally. And, we need the regulators to make certain that money transmitters and the banks are doing what the law requires. Finally, we need authorities here in the United States and abroad to make it more difficult for criminals and other lawbreakers to avoid proper scrutiny by conducting their financial affairs in offshore secrecy jurisdictions. These are difficult problems, and law enforcement needs all the help we can get.

Mr. ROHRABACHER. Thank you very much. I know we are going to have quite a few questions for you when we return, but maybe not as tough as questions we will have for Mr. Herde.

You may proceed, Mr. Herde.

## STATEMENT OF MR. MICHAEL HERDE, MANAGING DIRECTOR, REGION AMERICAS HEAD OF COMPLIANCE, UBS INVESTMENT BANK

Mr. HERDE. Mr. Chairman, thank you for inviting UBS to this hearing.

Mr. ROHRABACHER. Would you mind moving a little closer to the mike?

Mr. HERDE. Thank you for inviting UBS to this hearing. I am Michael Herde, Head of Compliance for the UBS Investment Bank in the Americas.

UBS is a New York Stock Exchange listed company with more than 26,000 employees in the Americas operating through 420 offices.

I will discuss our AML (Anti-Money Laundering) compliance program, our global sanctions policy, and our failings in connection with the ECI program.

Last year, we adopted an unparalleled worldwide economic sanctions policy. The policy combines EU, United States, UN and Swiss measures against companies, regimes, terrorists and others, and applies all of them globally to our businesses.

UBS operates a comprehensive anti-money laundering program. I would like to highlight three aspects of this program.

First, know your customer. Knowing your customer is the first line of defense in preventing money laundering. UBS does not accept business with accounts in fictitious names. It does not accept accounts with businesses that are shell companies and it does not accept business with money changers.

We have global standards on the identification of client beneficial ownership, on clients connected to higher risk countries, and on politically exposed persons. We seek to understand the source of each client's assets.

Second, monitoring. UBS has invested heavily in intelligent technology and human resources to implement our controls. This technology includes sophisticated monitoring tools designed to screen payments to comply with our sanctions policies and to identify suspicious transactions.

Third, culture of compliance. Our employees in the United States and all over the world appreciate the important role that financial institutions play in the prevention, detection and reporting of money laundering.

We provide regular training to employees and a firm-wide culture that emphasizes compliance with our policies and the law.

Mr. Chairman, I want to make clear that when we suspect money laundering activity we take action. We investigate the activity, report our suspicions, and we support law enforcement authorities all over the world in their investigations.

United States authorities, for example, may access Swiss Bank customer information through well established processes for mutual legal assistance. Senior United States officials have repeatedly observed that Swiss financial privacy laws are not an obstacle in the war on terror.

UBS is committed to being a strong ally in the fight against money laundering and terrorist financing. I would like to take a moment to discuss our failings in connection with the ECI program.

Between 1996 and 2003, UBS participated in the Federal Reserve Bank's Extended Custodial Inventory program. One aim of the ECI program was to exchange old U.S. bank notes for new ones, which are more difficult to counterfeit. UBS acted unacceptably in its operation of the ECI facility. Some former employees engaged in bank note transactions with countries that were subject to U.S. economic sanctions. These transactions were improper in light of our obligations to the Federal Reserve Bank of New York. UBS deeply regrets these failings.

UBS, with the assistance of Swiss counsel and United States counsel, conducted a full investigation and fully cooperated with the investigations of United States and Swiss authorities. Our investigation found no evidence that any of these bank note exchanges involved money laundering or terrorist financing.

UBS has learned a great deal from its ECI-related failings. First, we accepted full responsibility for the ECI matter and took severe disciplinary action, including dismissing several employees.

Second, we ended our international bank notes trading business.

Third, as you noted, we paid a $100 million civil penalty to the Federal Reserve and accepted additional inspections and a reprimand from the Swiss Federal Banking Commission. Our actions were the subject of comprehensive hearings in both the House and Senate in 2004.

More recently, UBS adopted a worldwide economic sanctions compliance program. Our new policy tracks economic sanctions imposed by the United States, Switzerland, the EU and the UN and applies them all globally to all of our businesses. We took this step for a number of reasons, including the increasing globalization of our business.

As a result, UBS has decided to exit business in Iran, Cuba, Syria, Sudan, North Korea, and Myanmar. Limited business, where permitted by law, including United States law, is accepted. No other non-U.S. bank has to our knowledge taken a similar step.

To conclude, Mr. Chairman, first, UBS deeply regrets its failings related to the ECI program. It has sought to learn from them. Second, UBS has developed what we believe is a leading global sanctions compliance program and is committed to maintaining a leading AML compliance program. Third, UBS is committed to participating effectively in the fight against money laundering and terrorist financing.

Thank you and I would be happy to answer any questions to the best of my ability.

[The prepared statement of Mr. Herde follows:]

PREPARED STATEMENT OF MR. MICHAEL HERDE, MANAGING DIRECTOR, REGION AMERICAS HEAD OF COMPLIANCE, UBS INVESTMENT BANK

Mr. Chairman, thank you for inviting UBS to participate in this hearing regarding international banks and their role in the global fight against money laundering. I am Michael Herde, a Managing Director and Head of Compliance for the Americas, at UBS' Investment Bank. Previously I was Head of Compliance for the Investment Bank in Europe, the Middle East and Africa, based in London. As you may know, Mr. Chairman, UBS AG is a financial institution incorporated in Switzerland and operating globally, including through over 420 offices in the U.S. UBS employs more than 70,000 employees globally, with over 26,000 in the U.S. In addition to investment banking, we offer wealth management, asset management, and business banking services. Our three primary regulators are the Swiss Federal Banking Commission, the Federal Reserve System, and the U.K.'s Financial Services Authority.

We are pleased to have the opportunity to discuss our firm's extensive anti-money laundering and compliance programs, and in particular, our groundbreaking global sanctions policy. In the words of our Chairman, Marcel Ospel,

> We recognize that for criminals to benefit from their crimes, the proceeds derived must be secure and accessible to them, and banks are naturally targeted to provide these services. Banks like UBS have long recognized the need for concerted action in denying criminals access to our services. We also recognize the more profound need to protect the integrity of the global financial system of which we form part.

September 2004

We believe that UBS' anti-money laundering policies and procedures are among the most stringent in the world. We know, however, we must always be looking for ways to further improve our operations as new threats are posed by those wishing to test the integrity of the world financial system. With this in mind, in 2005, we adopted an unparalleled, uniform, worldwide economic sanctions policy that combines U.S., E.U., U.N. and Swiss measures against countries, regimes, terrorists, narcotics traffickers, and proliferators of weapons of mass destruction. We apply these measures collectively and globally to all our businesses.

UBS' AML PROGRAM

UBS operates a comprehensive series of anti-money laundering controls focusing on key risk areas and dedicates substantial resources towards preventing criminals, corrupt officials, and terrorist financiers from using the firm's services. These compliance initiatives are designed to meet the highest international standards, including those established by the USA PATRIOT Act, the EU 3rd Money Laundering Directive, and the Swiss Money Laundering Ordinance.

I will highlight three primary areas that we focus on as we implement our programs:

1. *Know Your Customer:* Knowing our customers and their financial profiles is a critical first step in assessing our relationships with current and potential clients. As such, UBS does not accept business with anonymous accounts, accounts in fictitious names, or shell companies or trusts lacking transparency as to the beneficial owner. As part of our standard process, every effort is made to identify the source of account assets. We have global standards on the establishment of beneficial ownership and dedicated compliance teams focusing on clients connected to countries of higher risks and on Politically Exposed Persons. In short, we go to great lengths to know potential customers before deciding whether or not to do business with them.
2. *Monitoring and Intelligence:* We need the best intelligence to assess our current and potential customers. Therefore, UBS has made substantial investments in intelligent technology and human resources to implement our controls. This technology includes sophisticated monitoring tools designed to screen payments to comply with our sanctions policy and to identify suspicious transactions. UBS now employs approximately 1,750 legal and compliance professionals, of which a substantial number are focused primarily on money laundering prevention.
3. *Culture of Compliance:* Having the best policies is important, but they can only be truly effective by establishing a culture among our employees to embrace and implement these policies. Our employees in the United States and all over the world, from senior management on down, appreciate the important and unique role that financial institutions must play in the prevention, detection, and reporting of money laundering. We provide regular training of employees and a firm-wide culture that emphasizes compliance with our policies and the law.

UBS is a founding member of the Wolfsberg Group. The Wolfsberg Group is named after the UBS training center in Switzerland where, in 2000, groundbreaking global industry AML standards on private banking were formulated. The Wolfsberg Group is an association of twelve global financial institutions including Citigroup, Goldman Sachs and JP Morgan Chase, working together to develop state-of-the-art financial services industry standards in the areas of Anti-Money Laundering and controls to Counter Terrorist Financing. The Group has produced statements of industry standards on areas such as correspondent banking, suppression of financing of terrorism, and dealing with Politically Exposed Persons.

Mr. Chairman, I want to make clear that when we suspect money laundering activity, we take action. We investigate potential suspicious activity, file suspicious activity reports, and we support law enforcement authorities all over the world in providing requested banking information. UBS has no higher priority than to be a strong ally in the fight against money laundering and terrorist financing.

UBS fully supports law enforcement authorities around the world against money laundering and the war against terrorism. For example, U.S. authorities may obtain access to Swiss bank customer information through well-established, cross-border channels allowing for mutual legal assistance. As a result, senior U.S. officials have repeatedly observed that Swiss financial privacy laws are not an obstacle in the war on terror. For example, speaking in the wake of September 11, 2001, former U.S. Attorney General John Ashcroft said:

> The Swiss banking system is well known as an example to the world. But one of the myths once held around the world was that the system was somehow incapable of acting to support law enforcement against terrorists and organized crime. That myth has been dispelled by the constructive conduct of the Swiss government and the Swiss banking system.
>
> Switzerland is an intersection on the world's financial highways, and Switzerland operates this intersection very responsibly.
>
> The world should take note of the responsible way in which the Swiss have acted . . . The world is a safer place because of the Swiss approach.[1]

UBS welcomes the close working relationship it has developed with U.S., Swiss, and other law enforcement authorities, and we will continue to support their efforts.

---

[1] John Ashcroft, Press conference in Bern, 12 June 2002

ECI PROGRAM FAILURES

Our commitment to build a cooperative relationship with U.S. banking regulators is evident in the work undertaken by our senior management in 2003 and 2004 in response to the discovery of failures in our administration of a contract with the Federal Reserve Bank of New York. From March 1996 through October 2003, under a contract with the Federal Reserve, UBS participated in the Extended Custodial Inventory Program, known as ECI. The ECI has several purposes, one of which is to exchange old U.S. banknotes, held internationally, for new U.S. banknotes, which are more difficult to counterfeit.

UBS acted unacceptably in operating its ECI facility. In breach of the ECI contract, some of our employees engaged in banknote transactions with countries that were subject to U.S. economic sanctions. UBS deeply regrets these failures.

Upon learning of this problem, our senior management instituted its own internal investigation and fully cooperated with the investigations underway by the U.S. and Swiss authorities.

Our investigation has found no evidence that any of these banknote exchanges involved money laundering or terrorist financing.

Our firm has learned a great deal from its ECI-related challenges. We have committed ourselves to enacting the proper remedies to correct our deficiencies and improve our compliance programs.

First, we accepted full responsibility for the ECI matter and we instituted severe disciplinary actions, including dismissing several employees.

Second, we ended our international banknotes trading business.

Third, UBS was sanctioned by our U.S. and Swiss regulators. We paid a $100 million civil penalty to the Federal Reserve and accepted additional inspections and a reprimand from the Swiss Federal Banking Commission. Our actions were the subject of two comprehensive hearings in both the House and Senate in 2004.

More recently, UBS adopted a uniform worldwide economic sanctions compliance policy. Our new policy tracks economic sanctions imposed by the United States, Switzerland, the European Union, and the resolutions of the United Nations' Security Council. It applies them collectively and globally in all of our businesses in all jurisdictions in which we operate.

As part of this unique initiative, UBS has made the business decision to exit business in Iran, Cuba, Syria, Sudan, North Korea, and Myanmar, with limited exceptions and only where they are permitted by law, including U.S. law. Permissible transactions include activities that are specifically authorized by law or exempt from the economic sanctions: for example, financial transactions in support of authorized humanitarian work by international organizations in Sudan.

To conclude, Mr. Chairman:

First, UBS deeply regrets its failures relating to the ECI program.

Second, we have developed what we believe is a leading global sanctions compliance program, and we are committed to maintaining one of the most stringent AML programs in the industry.

Third, UBS is committed to being an effective participant in the fight against money laundering and terrorist financing, supporting efforts to prevent use of the international banking system to further illicit activities.

Thank you for your attention to our testimony today, I will be pleased to respond to any questions you may have.

Mr. ROHRABACHER. How long have you been with UBS?

Mr. HERDE. I joined the bank in January 1999.

Mr. ROHRABACHER. So about 6 years, 7 years now?

Mr. HERDE. Yes, sir.

Mr. ROHRABACHER. All right. Thank you.

I will proceed with a few questions here.

Mr. Middlemiss, you have charged several of these banks with crimes and you have actually convicted and had recent convictions. You talked about $100 million that went from Brazil into this bank in New York and then it was headed for Vietnam.

What happened to the money?

Mr. MIDDLEMISS. Well, first of all, Mr. Chairman, with respect to money coming from Brazil and going to Vietnam, let me just clarify that those two sets of cases are not linked, they are two separate cases, each of which involved money remitters.

Mr. ROHRABACHER. Okay. When you get a bad guy and you have found somebody trying to transfer money, what happens to the money?

Mr. MIDDLEMISS. Well, I can give you two examples. With respect to the money that went to Vietnam, to state the obvious, the $132 million that was transmitted went to Vietnam. In fact, money remissions I think is perhaps the second largest component of the Vietnamese economy. So, for example——

Mr. ROHRABACHER. Let us not move on. So Vietnam is now becoming a destination place for dirty money? Is that right?

Mr. MIDDLEMISS. I think the point is, Mr. Chairman, that we do not know how much of the $132 million is dirty or not dirty. It would be unfair to say that the entire amount is in fact dirty. The problem and the E felony——

Mr. ROHRABACHER. We do know that it is not transparent, right? They are seeking to go through New York and other ways to try to make this not transparent.

Mr. MIDDLEMISS. This is the gravamen of the offense. The business itself is prosecuted because it is illegally moving the money and not keeping to the regulatory requirements.

Mr. ROHRABACHER. The chances of it, it is possible that somebody just does not want to pay their taxes, but it is also possible that this could be really dirty money. This could be organized crime, gangster money from Brazil, drug money, any number of things, or it could be just somebody not wanting to pay their taxes, but it is still dirty money.

Mr. MIDDLEMISS. Yes, that is exactly the point. And it is very difficult because these corrupt enterprises do not keep the proper records to drill down and get to the ultimate person who is transferring the money and to identify the reasons why.

Mr. ROHRABACHER. So to go back to the question, is Vietnam becoming a center for receiving dirty money?

Mr. MIDDLEMISS. I certainly cannot tell based on the data that I have in front of me, based on these cases. I can tell you that it is fair to infer that large sums of money, we know not from where, are being sent to Vietnam. I can tell you that I suspect that businesses in New York may well be funneling off their assets and not paying taxes on the money that they earn and sending it directly and secretly to Vietnam.

Mr. ROHRABACHER. And now what we need to do also, then, is find out how many banks in Switzerland or other places get transactions from Vietnam, right?

Mr. MIDDLEMISS. Well, I think what you are leading me to is that I would have no idea how to do that because I would not be able to get records from the Vietnamese bank.

Mr. ROHRABACHER. Right. Correct. And, again, back to the dirty money idea, let us say you get somebody and you finally have got them, their money is somewhere, it is probably in some bank somewhere, does the bank end up with the money? You do not know how much it is, you do not know——

Mr. MIDDLEMISS. The banks that we have looked at and the tools that we have in New York are slightly different than those available to Federal prosecutors. For example, one of the money remitters, going back to the Brazilian set of cases, was a company called

Transmar and essentially it was a doleiro in Brazil. It was in the business of helping its Brazilian clients illegally move money out of Brazil. The money went into the New York Transmar account, and millions of dollars flowed through the account. Sometimes, the money went to other dollar dealers. Sometimes, it went offshore to the Caribbean. Sometimes it went to other accounts, but at the end of the day, when we got to the account, despite the fact that—I think the amount is listed I my remarks, but millions of dollars had flowed through the account, we were left with $158,000 that we could seize.

Mr. ROHRABACHER. I see.

Mr. MIDDLEMISS. There was no money there.

Mr. ROHRABACHER. The rest of the money is off in the electronic world of somebody's account somewhere.

Mr. MIDDLEMISS. Exactly.

Mr. ROHRABACHER. In the never never land of international banking.

Mr. MIDDLEMISS. What we have tried to do is shut one of the windows through which that money can flow.

Mr. ROHRABACHER. I guess what I am asking you, can we assume that some banks have ended up with a lot of money throughout this process, in the process and in the end?

Mr. MIDDLEMISS. Yes.

Mr. ROHRABACHER. How much? We are saying a lot of money, let us say $100 million, how much of it is going to end up—can you estimate? Even if they are not caught, of course, you have a certain amount of money that is being made by the client and banks are making profit all the way along the line on this, right? That is why they are doing it. They would not be doing it because it is a public service.

Mr. MIDDLEMISS. Yes, I think that with each particular transaction that takes place, there is a fee. But also, for example, with Israel Discount Bank of New York, one of the reasons why these transactions were enabled was so that the bank itself could grow its presence in South America—so that it could facilitate transactions with people that they wanted to have other relationships with, perhaps more profitable ones, such as loaning them money, rather than merely doing them the service of wiring their money from place to place.

Mr. ROHRABACHER. So we have people at these financial institutions who are making money and that is off bad money, so to speak, but then we have bad guys who the reason they want to sometimes take money from one place to another is so they can accomplish evil things, like blowing up buildings or destroying people in certain places that they do not like them or growing poppies or cocoa or whatever, which is all facilitated by this transfer.

Mr. MIDDLEMISS. That is correct. And, again, it is hard to get to the ultimate bad guy, although because we have been able to share information with our Brazilian colleagues, our Brazilian prosecutors and police officers have taken information that we have developed in New York and successfully prosecuted a lot of bad guys in Brazil.

Mr. ROHRABACHER. So we have a lot of folks in $2000 suits and driving fancy sports cars, pillars of their community in different parts of the world who are bankers but are really accomplices in some of the most horrific crimes we could imagine. Is that correct?

Mr. MIDDLEMISS. I do not think that is an unfair statement. Yes.

Mr. ROHRABACHER. All right. That is all I needed to hear.

Let us get over to Mr. Herde now.

Nothing of what I just said needs to reflect badly on you or your bank, first of all, let me note, but let me ask about a specific thing.

Your bank was fined $100 million for violating the Extended Custodial Inventory program. Now, can you explain to me why the employees of your bank chose to violate the program? What did they expect to get out of it? Why would they do that?

Mr. HERDE. The investigation that was conducted with both United States and Swiss outside counsel reached the conclusion that none of the employees involved stood to gain personally in a pecuniary way from their transgression.

Mr. ROHRABACHER. That makes it even more damning on the bank, I might add. If they did not do it for their own personal gain, you would understand that they were gaming their employer, but they must have thought that your bank was going to be the beneficiary, then.

Mr. HERDE. At best, the investigation reached the conclusion that those employees had the misunderstanding, I should say, that operational efficiencies in the short term would be in the interests of the bank. Those employees have been fired. Our senior management has definitively spoken and made clear that operational shortcuts are not an acceptable means of advancing the bank's business.

Mr. ROHRABACHER. Why would they think it would be in the interests of your bank?

Mr. HERDE. They thought they were saving some money.

Mr. ROHRABACHER. Saving some money?

Mr. HERDE. They thought that by conducting the ECI facility in the way that they did they were saving literally tiny sums of money in operational processes.

Mr. ROHRABACHER. What was the level of business that your bank held in Iran and Cuba outside of the ECI program?

Mr. HERDE. Specifically—I am not sure if I can recall specifically the total amounts. If you took all the countries where there are U.S. economic sanctions involved and put them together, whether by assets or revenues, it would amount to about 1/20 of 1 percent of our overall business, so it is a tiny sum.

The scale of businesses outside of the ECI program relative even to these particular areas were 1.5 percent of——

Mr. ROHRABACHER. But in terms of your management of that program, this was a huge percentage of those particular accounts. Maybe a minuscule amount of the overall accounts, but of these two accounts, Iran and Cuba, what we have here is probably—because they are so minuscule in relationship to the ECI, the ECI must have been a significant part of your dealings with them, right?

Mr. HERDE. Certainly there were large volumes of transactions with those two countries or the banks in those two countries through and related to the ECI program.

Mr. ROHRABACHER. And then would not these employees who lost their jobs, they were the ones who were just in charge of those two countries for the ECI account, right?

Mr. HERDE. No, sir. The ECI program as administered by the U.S. Government sought to recirculate new U.S. dollar bills into the international economy. Our business, I think, was $170 billion. I think that we did. And we did that with France, Germany, Italy, Spain. Also Cuba, also Iran. That was wrong, no question. And the individuals who were involved in doing this operational business on a day-to-day business did the whole program, ECI, non-ECI, all of the physical bank notes trading business.

Mr. ROHRABACHER. Well, were the employees that we are talking about here, were they trying to protect UBS's business outside of the ECI program by giving these bank notes to Iran and Cuba? Was there some sort of business that they were trying to promote or to protect that your bank is involved in in order to transfer these notes? Was there any indication of that?

Mr. HERDE. The best and most solid indication that we have is that—and this is what the investigation, I believe, found, was that the employees thought that they were gaining some operational efficiencies primarily.

Mr. ROHRABACHER. But not necessarily protecting investments in other economic activities that the bank was involved in in Cuba and Iran.

Mr. HERDE. I do not think there has been any evidence to suggest that there is a linkage between these businesses and the other businesses.

Mr. ROHRABACHER. I will return. I have used more than my time, but we will have a second round of questioning.

Mr. Delahunt, go right ahead.

We have been joined by Mr. Royce, Chairman of the Terrorism and Non-Proliferation Subcommittee.

We appreciate your presence here, Ed.

Mr. ROYCE. Thank you, Mr. Chairman.

We will have Mr. Delahunt now and proceed.

Mr. DELAHUNT. Mr. Middlemiss, it would appear to me, and I guess I am stating the obvious, that the significant issue here is the issue of secrecy and lack of transparency. In your experience, has there been any improvement in terms of the international relationships that currently exist in terms of more transparency?

Mr. MIDDLEMISS. In terms of more transparency?

Mr. DELAHUNT. Are we trending in the right direction, I guess is the question. I know there exists a convention, but reading your testimony and that of Mr. Moscow and recognizing the experience that you have, how do we go about achieving the level of transparency that would be necessary so that the issue of money laundering and our concerns, which are justifiable, would be obviated? Give me the solution.

Mr. MIDDLEMISS. I wish I could do that. I wish there was an easy answer and I think if there was one, someone smarter than me would have already given you that answer. I can talk about the importance of information such as the beneficial owner of a trust needing to be available. I can talk to you about the importance of there not being bearer share corporations and suggesting to you that——

Mr. DELAHUNT. But this would have to be achieved in conjunction with other nations, it would have to be done via a new international convention. Is that a fair statement?

Mr. MIDDLEMISS. I think it would be, or one of the ones that exist presently.

Mr. DELAHUNT. Amending or enhancing?

Mr. MIDDLEMISS. Right. But certainly asking a prosecutor in New York now to do our job, which essentially is to trace the money, in the current international climate—that is impossible to do.

Mr. DELAHUNT. That is the reality. It is impossible.

Mr. MIDDLEMISS. There are significant difficulties tracing money around the world——

Mr. DELAHUNT. Particularly if we have hostile relationships with another nation state.

Mr. MIDDLEMISS. Not necessarily even hostile relations, but you still have to go through an inordinate amount of paperwork and time to get the most basic records out of certain countries.

Mr. DELAHUNT. Just for the record, I would note that under Section 311 of the USA PATRIOT Act, there have been eight international banks that have received so-called special measures, one in Macau, two in Latvia, First Merchant Bank of the Turkish Republic of Northern Cyprus, the Info Bank of Belarus, a bank in Syria, a bank in Lebanon, a bank in Burma, the Asian Wealth Bank, and the jurisdictions we are talking about are Burma in November 2003, Ukraine in 2002, and I did not even know that this nation existed, Nauruo in December 2002. As the Chairman indicated in his remarks, he was going to be educated, but I can only see this issue being resolved by an agreement on an international level to enhance transparency and removing these impediments that allow the kind of progress, I think, that we all would embrace.

Have you had any dealings with OFAC?

Mr. MIDDLEMISS. Not directly, no.

Mr. DELAHUNT. Okay. Let me ask you a question. Is it customary for a wholly-owned subsidiary of a U.S. company to use offshore banks essentially as a mail drop for their purposes?

Mr. MIDDLEMISS. I cannot speak as to whether or not it is customary, although I believe I can think of an example where I saw something at least very similar to that.

Mr. DELAHUNT. If you could, then, relate that example. I am referring, of course, to the use of—I guess it was the Cayman Islands for a subsidiary of Halliburton to be utilized, I guess, according to this report, as a mail drop for the parent company of Halliburton.

Mr. MIDDLEMISS. I am not familiar with that particular fact pattern, although I can give you an example of a similar situation.

Mr. DELAHUNT. As a prosecutor, would that raise concerns for you, whether there was a potential violation of the sanctions law?

Mr. MIDDLEMISS. Is that something that I would look at?

Mr. DELAHUNT. Yes.

Mr. MIDDLEMISS. I think as a New York County prosecutor, perhaps not. As a Federal prosecutor, I would hope so.

Mr. DELAHUNT. As a Federal prosecutor, you would hope so. If in fact at that particular office in the Cayman Islands, if there was nobody there—let me give you a hypothetical. If there was nobody there, there was an office and a telephone and the phone never rang and mail was forwarded to the parent company that was headquartered or at least had an office in Dubai, and we are familiar with Dubai, we have been reading about Dubai for the past month or so, and this company was doing business in Iran, a rogue state, providing some $40 million worth of services to enhance their ability in the energy field, and the law stated that the subsidiary had to operate independently, and that is the legal term, would you infer that maybe the parent company was operating there rather than the subsidiary and that the subsidiary was a fiction and that this company was doing business with a rogue nation, a member of the Axis of Evil club? Would that come to your mind?

Mr. MIDDLEMISS. I think it is an issue——

Mr. DELAHUNT. If you were a Federal prosecutor, Mr. Middlemiss.

Mr. MIDDLEMISS. Well, actually, with respect to being a state prosecutor, the issues that you raise are very similar to ones that involve the Enron case, where certain entities that were shams were used to take part in transactions that were designed to bolster Enron's books and records in real ways.

Mr. DELAHUNT. Right. Right.

Mr. MIDDLEMISS. With respect to the issue of the subsidiary, I cannot speak to it.

Mr. DELAHUNT. I cannot, either. I would like to hear, though, from representatives of the parent company and the subsidiary, but I have a strong suspicion that I will not have an opportunity to ask a representatives of either Halliburton or Halliburton's subsidiary that was doing business to the tune of tens of millions of dollars with a rogue state, but with that I will yield back.

Mr. ROHRABACHER. Thank you very much.

If somebody is transferring $100 million from Brazil to a bank in New York and then it goes on to Vietnam, how much money does the bank in New York make on doing that?

Mr. MIDDLEMISS. I cannot state with specificity, Mr. Chairman, but I can say that with respect to wire transfers I believe that banks make a very small amount of money based on that business alone.

Mr. ROHRABACHER. Okay. So you are not talking about $10 million to transfer $100 million, you may be talking about $100,000?

Mr. MIDDLEMISS. No, I do not think so. I think it is less than that.

Mr. ROHRABACHER. Less than that?

Mr. MIDDLEMISS. Less than that. Yes.

Mr. ROHRABACHER. All right.

Ileana?

Ms. ROS-LEHTINEN. Thank you so much.

Mr. Rohrabacher, thank you very much for letting me participate in your Subcommittee hearing on this important topic and I look forward to being a part of the upcoming hearings as well.

Mr. Herde, I had some questions for you. In your testimony before us today and in your written testimony as well, you use these exact phrases: Its failings, its failures, acted unacceptably, improper actions, deficiencies. Then, after Mr. Rohrabacher's questions, you used the phrase operational shortcuts, and finally the word wrong. Nowhere is the word illegal.

Did you pay a $100 million for deficiencies, shortcuts, or were you paying a fine because of illegal transactions? Was UBS breaking the law?

Mr. HERDE. We owed certain obligations to the Federal Reserve Bank of New York. Those obligations——

Ms. ROS-LEHTINEN. Did UBS commit an illegal act when it was involved in these ECI transactions with OFAC sanctioned countries? Was it illegal for UBS to be involved in these operations?

Mr. HERDE. Non-United States banks and foreign incorporated subsidiaries of United States banks may permissibly engage in transactions, for example, with Iran. Had UBS conducted those transactions away from its ECI program, it would not have violated its obligations.

Ms. ROS-LEHTINEN. Why is it that you paid a $100 million civil penalty to the Federal Reserve and accepted the reprimand?

Mr. HERDE. Because we undertook certain obligations to the Federal Reserve Bank in New York and we failed to meet those obligations and that is a very serious matter. We also——

Ms. ROS-LEHTINEN. Were there two sets of books, one internal that UBS had, where, I imagine, the reports have indicated you kept good records of what Cuba was sending and other countries that are sanctioned countries that could not participate in this program—one set of internal records and another set of records that were given to the Federal regulators? Were there two sets of records?

Mr. HERDE. There was one set of records, but there was a series of false reports submitted by the bank staff that——

Ms. ROS-LEHTINEN. False reports. Is that an illegal activity? Where does the word illegal come into play with what is going on? And I hope that it is in the past tense, but I am not so sure. It is so hard to pinpoint you and it has been so difficult after so many months to have you say what it is that you were involved with. And I do not mean you personally.

Mr. HERDE. Of course.

Ms. ROS-LEHTINEN. I meant the institution you represent.

Mr. HERDE. Of course. I stand here on behalf of UBS. There is no question. UBS is not happy with its conduct.

Ms. ROS-LEHTINEN. Not happy with its conduct. Well, what kind of conduct was it? Illegal conduct?

Mr. HERDE. We failed to meet our obligations to the Fed.

Ms. ROS-LEHTINEN. Failed to meet the obligations. So when the Federal regulators were investigating UBS, the level of cooperation by UBS, months and months and months of pushing UBS for money laundering, terrorism financing, illegally using the ECI program, having different books, and then UBS has the position that it was some minor employees, eight employees, perhaps, and they were fired and that the problem is taken care of.

If we could go back to the relationship between the ECI program and other business dealings with Cuba, for example, you are saying that you did not pursue ECI programs with the regime in the hope of getting more business out of it with Cuba or any other rogue states?

Are you saying that you are satisfied with UBS's relationship with the Castro regime and does that mean that UBS had an extensive relationship with Cuban entities and the regime?

What is the nature or what was the nature of this transaction? Can I ask you again, did UBS employees violate the ECI program with the intent of enhancing UBS business relationships with Iran, Cuba or other rogue regimes?

Mr. HERDE. As I believe I indicated previously, the investigation concluded that a primary driver for the activity by the individuals who were involved was a misguided perception that operational efficiencies would be in the interests of the institution.

Ms. ROS-LEHTINEN. Misguided perception that operational efficiencies? I just want to make sure—misguided perception by the employees of UBS who were doing that transaction?

Mr. HERDE. Yes.

Mr. ROHRABACHER. The Chairman would like to interrupt. That does sound like very suspicious language, pardon me for being a former journalist, but when I hear a corporate representative use that description, I would be very suspicious of it.

Mr. HERDE. Let me be quite clear. UBS is not proud of its failings in connection with the ECI program. I use that word quite deliberately. We failed. We believe that we have taken responsibility. We have settled with the United States Government. We have cooperated with all inquiries. We have settled with the Swiss Government. And we believe that we have taken a number of corrective actions, including most recently the introduction of a unique global economic sanctions program which we do not believe any other non-U.S. bank has undertaken.

We also believe, and I would note, that foreign incorporated subsidiaries of U.S. banks can engage in activities with Iran in the same way that non-U.S. banks can.

Ms. ROS-LEHTINEN. Thank you.

I wanted to ask you about operational efficiency. If what you are saying is that these eight employees or so were dealing with OFAC sanctioned countries knowingly, they knew that these countries were countries that should not have participated in the ECI program, no doubt, why was dealing with them a way to get to operational efficiency? What is that operational shortcut? I do not understand how dealing with sanctioned companies was a way of getting to operational—this is your phrase, operational efficiency.

What about those transactions would lead one to operational efficiency?

Mr. HERDE. There was a way that UBS could have set up its business operations that would have involved duplicate sets of bank notes businesses: One a completely ECI-compliant business and the other, the non-U.S. bank, foreign bank note dealing operation. In the same way that other international banks today deal with these countries and re-transmit the bank notes to the U.S. Government, UBS could have done that. For whatever improper reason, the employees involved did not do that and they have been held responsible for that and anybody who was involved in both those activities and the——

Ms. ROS-LEHTINEN. Anyone involved in those activities, in addition to those employees that are at the lower level, would you state that no administration or higher officials in UBS knowingly participated in these illegal transactions, that it was only these eight individuals and no one higher up than that?

Mr. HERDE. I am satisfied that appropriate disciplinary action, including termination or separation from employment, was taken against all individuals who had an active hand in either——

Ms. ROS-LEHTINEN. What about an inactive hand? What about someone who might have known about the transaction? See, we are being led to believe that these individuals did it on their own for operational shortcuts and for operational efficiencies and not to enhance UBS's dealing with Iran, Cuba and other sanctioned countries. It is hard to believe that others did not know.

Mr. HERDE. You are correct. Actually, individuals who had knowledge but were not involved in the process at all were also fired.

Ms. ROS-LEHTINEN. How many individuals were fired as a result of this illegal activity?

Mr. HERDE. Fired and separated from employment, right? Two slightly different categories. I do not know. Between eight, ten, eleven in total. There were some people who were fired outright and there were some people who left the bank.

Ms. ROS-LEHTINEN. So how many of them were fired and how many of them left the bank?

Mr. HERDE. I would be happy to go back and provide that information.

Ms. ROS-LEHTINEN. I do not have a very good track record with UBS in providing me any information, so we can say fine and I will not be holding my breath.

Mr. ROHRABACHER. Ileana——

Ms. ROS-LEHTINEN. Just one more question.

Mr. ROHRABACHER. Certainly, but if I could amplify?

Ms. ROS-LEHTINEN. Oh, yes. Go right ahead.

Mr. ROHRABACHER. Was your answer that individuals with knowledge were disciplined or is your answer all individuals with knowledge were disciplined, higher up?

Mr. HERDE. To the best of my knowledge and belief, right? To the best of my knowledge and belief, all the individuals who had knowledge of the ongoing activities are no longer working for the bank.

Mr. ROHRABACHER. All right. And the caveat to the best of my knowledge was certainly a good caveat for you.

Go right ahead.

Ms. ROS-LEHTINEN. Thank you, Mr. Chairman.

I am interested, Mr. Middlemiss, the bank says they have a few employees who were involved in the transaction, the higher ups did not know, they were fired or left their employment, whatever phrase you want to use, the bank pays $100 million in fines and that is it. Do we have a system in prosecution for if you have a lot of money you pay your way out of whatever problems, whatever—let me see, what was the phrase? Whatever operational shortcuts you were involved with, whatever unacceptable behaviors, whatever deficiencies, whatever failures, you pay a fine, $100 million, that is it. You can pay to get out of trouble, do not have to face any criminal charges.

Is there an ongoing criminal investigation of UBS's misconduct in the ECI program that you know of?

Mr. MIDDLEMISS. I do not know, Congresswoman.

Ms. ROS-LEHTINEN. Well, who would be handling that?

Mr. MIDDLEMISS. I would think the Department of Justice, if there is one.

Ms. ROS-LEHTINEN. And I know that Mr. Morgenthau has taken on some big cases in the past. Do you have right now in the New York County any open investigations of UBS's transactions related to any of the items that we have discussed?

Mr. MIDDLEMISS. I do not think I can speak to that.

Ms. ROS-LEHTINEN. All right. I know I have taken up a lot of time. I have a lot of other questions.

Mr. ROHRABACHER. We may have a second round.

Ms. ROS-LEHTINEN. Thank you.

Mr. ROHRABACHER. Mr. Royce, you may proceed.

Mr. ROYCE. Thank you, Mr. Chairman.

Obviously, there have been some questionable transactions brought to light here today and, indeed, I think bank examiners at the Fed and at the OCC (Office of the Comptroller of the Currency) have become much more aggressive about potential money laundering activities by U.S. regulated banks.

Additionally, the Financial Services Committee, the other Committee that I serve on, has spent a great deal of time reviewing anti-money laundering enforcement issues.

With that said, presently, I am concerned about proactive measures banks and the regulatory community are taking to prevent future transactions and transgressions of these types.

Today, we have heard from one bank as to what corrective measures they have taken to help combat money laundering, including closing its bank note trading operations, its new global sanctions policy, and a closer working relationship with United States- and Swiss-based regulators.

I would ask what measures have major international banks taken to combat money laundering? In other words, are the major financial institutions that are domiciled in Europe following United States anti-money laundering prohibitions?

What are we doing to put leverage on that and how do we exert such leverage? Mr. Middlemiss?

Mr. MIDDLEMISS. With respect to what banks are doing in Europe, Mr. Royce, I do not think I am positioned to speak to that. What I hope does happen from the cases that have been investigated and prosecuted by the DA's office is that we bring attention to the importance of the underlying measures that already exist in terms of antimoney laundering controls in the United States. I hope that that sends a message to banks that are based elsewhere that do business here that the United States takes that regime seriously. And I hope that a message that we can tell them is that real application of the KYC (Know Your Customer) rules, filing suspicious activity reports and CTRs works. And one of the things we can tell those financial institutions, both abroad and here, is that when the do diligently filed suspicious activity reports, it works. People do read them. The Manhattan DA's office, for example, has prosecuted many cases, the basis of which the start of were suspicious activity reports themselves.

So I hope that that, to some extent, answers at least part of your question regarding what, if anything, we can do to encourage banks to—I do not want to say do better, but to live up to the regulatory regimes presently in existence.

Mr. ROYCE. Mr. Herde, did you have anything to add to that?

Mr. HERDE. Thank you very much, Congressman. I would suggest that the global standard that UBS has to acquire the identification of beneficial ownership is a key control and one that is in place in the EU and in Switzerland and is an expectation here in America. I think a suggestion would be rigorous application of that discipline to account opening.

Mr. ROYCE. And just for a moment, how would we expand that to application worldwide? In your view, Mr. Middlemiss, can you think of any way to make certain that the EU and the US——

Mr. MIDDLEMISS. I think that Mr. Delahunt touched on it before, Mr. Royce, in that it requires international cooperation to create a regime worldwide where everyone is playing by the same rules. If we do that, we would have success. How to do that is not a question I can answer.

Mr. ROYCE. Moving over to some of our efforts that gave rise to some of the laws that brought us to where we are today was the attempt to choke off the flow of funds used by various terrorist networks around the globe. Al-Qaeda, in particular, no longer has its finance committee operational but, on the other hand, in its place are small cells that move resources to radical terrorist organizations around the country, and that, it seems to me, can only be confronted through international cooperation in addition to applying our laws here.

But one of the issues that I think is going to beset us is what we go about Gulf state societies that move that money through terror finance. Some in those societies move a great deal of money, in the hundreds of millions of dollars, in some cases billions, that go through madrassas, the educational institutions across West Africa, North Africa, and Central Asia, in which the next generation of al-Qaeda operatives will be graduates once they learn jihad in those institutions.

One of the real questions is how the international community gets enough leverage on Saudi Arabia and other Gulf states to make certain that they get the transparency necessary so that we know where this money is being moved. The only way I can think this is going to happen is by elevating a position in transparency of an under secretary with enough power to sit on the IMF (International Monetary Fund) and World Bank and every other international institution where we have a presence with basically the exercise of the veto power against that state that will not force compliance with its financial institutions to these international standards.

That is going to take a much more robust and aggressive posture on the part of your department and on, frankly, the part of the Administration and Congress and the EU in order to make certain that we all reach the common agreement that unless we see compliance out of the Gulf states that are the originators of most of the money—there are prominent families in these societies that fund these types of activities—until we see a system that brings enough pressure on those governments so that those governments decide to enforce transparency through their own banking regulations, we are not going to be able to get to the root of the problem, and I would just like your observations on that Mr. Middlemiss.

Mr. MIDDLEMISS. Mr. Royce, I have to say that, as a local prosecutor, we prosecute the crimes that we see. In terms of help to do that, the international cooperative efforts and regime that you describe would be most helpful. Again, how to create that, as a local prosecutor, I do not think it is for me to opine on that.

Mr. ROYCE. And I guess my last question, since you are on the front lines, is how you feel the cooperation is going with foreign governments in terms of the assistance given you, the information and the tools that you need in real time in order to track this. Do you feel you are getting full cooperation, or could you point to any countries or principalities or any islands where you are not getting that assistance?

Mr. MIDDLEMISS. I can only speak anecdotally. I can say that the cooperation that we have had with Brazilian authorities has been excellent. In terms of getting information, Mr. Morgenthau has praised in the past the Channel Islands for their cooperation and the Isle of Mann. On the other hand, jurisdictions such as the Caymans and the Bahamas, in my experience, have been particularly problematic.

Mr. ROYCE. Bad actors. Can you think of a way that we could change our laws, or the international banking community could change their laws, to make it the case that banks would not want to open branches there or that individuals would not want to risk laundering their money through their branches? Is there a way that we could move in concert to make it very, very difficult for any bank to operate in the two countries that you just cited?

Mr. MIDDLEMISS. Again, as a matter of policy, Mr. Royce, I am hoping that some of the panelists who are going to come after me will have specific answers to that question. In terms of making other sovereign nations provide information required, that, again, becomes an issue of national politics.

Mr. ROYCE. But we can add into that the branching of banks doing business in the United States that branch into the Cayman Islands, and that is where I think the nexus may exist for us to put certain conditions on operations in the United States and in Europe, which would then dictate what kinds of operations could exist for branches in these countries.

Mr. MIDDLEMISS. There are laws presently in New York with respect to subpoena practice that if you are a branch of a foreign bank doing business in New York, and we serve you with a subpoena, you get into a conflict-of-laws question, where the bank can either produce documents that are located abroad, but doing so might violate that other nation's law. On the other hand, if they do not produce the documents in New York, and the corporate structure is such that they are a branch, they are going to violate New York law.

So the way, as a prosecutor, you like to think about it is that you are providing a choice to the financial institution. You can comply with New York law, or you can choose not to do business in New York. Now, unfortunately, the way that these decisions get made in the real world is a lot more complicated than that, because asking a major financial institution to leave New York is a question that probably is not going to be answered in the context of in the matter of an investigation of the business affairs of John Doe.

Mr. ROYCE. That is why we have oversight, and that is why we have an opportunity for you, Mr. Middlemiss, to raise that issue and for us to consider changing the laws and bringing the leverage and moving in concert. The EU is on the Hill today, and we certainly are going to have the opportunity later today with some of the EU members to talk about some of the issues that you brought up. Mr. Chairman, thank you.

Mr. ROHRABACHER. We certainly appreciate your leadership, Mr. Royce, in trying to find some specific reforms that will help protect us against terrorists using our international financial institutions as a vehicle to achieve their own objectives, their own blood objectives, I might add. So I appreciate your personal involvement in this issue.

Mr. ROYCE. Thank you, Mr. Chairman.

Mr. ROHRABACHER. We will have a very short round. Everybody will have about 1 minute to ask a couple of questions just in follow up, and that will be the end.

I would like to note that I know Ileana has had trouble about getting subpoenas fulfilled and paid attention to. Let me note that we cannot sometimes even get the President to pay attention to our appeals and things like that. So we have got a lot of work to do when it comes to making sure that the legislative branch has the information that we need, and, again, we appreciate Mr. Herde and your bank for being here to answer these questions. That is, again, a sign of good faith, and we appreciate that.

Do you have another minute or so?

Mr. DELAHUNT. I do, Mr. Chairman. Let me just associate myself with the import of the questions that were posed by my friend from California, Mr. Royce. I think he is headed in the right direction. It is an international problem, and unless we can get people on the same page, and we should be utilizing our leverage. I would hope that the United States, through the Administration, would have leverage with the Cayman Islands, for example.

What I would suggest to my friend is that, you know, whether it be financial services or whatever, we design our own good guy/bad guy list based upon the testimony and the input from those prosecutors.

But before you leave, Mr. Middlemiss, my colleague from Florida, Ms. Ros-Lehtinen, or maybe it was the Chairman, asked a question about existing investigations relative to UBS, and you said, I cannot comment. I just want to kind of clarify that a bit. I presume that you are restricted by the canons of ethics about commenting upon any investigations.

Mr. MIDDLEMISS. Yes, sir.

Mr. DELAHUNT. Okay. Am I hearing you right?

Mr. MIDDLEMISS. You should not infer one way or the other from my answer what investigation, if any, we have.

Mr. DELAHUNT. I do agree that we should have an answer to that question, and I do not know if there is anyone here from OFAC, but I think that they would be an appropriate agency, and I think the gentlelady deserves to have an answer. So is there anybody here from OFAC? We do not have anybody monitoring this hearing, but I know, Mr. Chairman, in the future that you will ensure that we have a representative of OFAC so we can determine how efficient and effective—it would be good to hear from the Administration in this regard.

One final question for you, Mr. Herde. You are out of the business of any relationship with the Government of Iran?

Mr. HERDE. We are in the process of exiting all of our business with clients and others in Iran. It is not a complete process.

Mr. DELAHUNT. What about Cuba?

Mr. HERDE. The same.

Mr. DELAHUNT. Because there was a statement made by the CEO of Halliburton that they, too, were going to exit from their relationship with Iran, and yet they kind of left a little bit of wiggle room, and I want to know if you are in the same position. Are you going to leave some wiggle room? To let me quote the CEO here, Mr. Leser, he said, "If the United States sanctions are lifted in the future or . . .," and this is what I find rather interesting, "more of our customers go there, we will return to this market." Is that the same position that you hold? Are you out of Iran and Cuba permanently?

Mr. HERDE. Yes. And to answer specifically related to Cuba, that relationship is terminated and gone and finished, and we have no intention of revisiting our policy as it now stands.

Mr. ROHRABACHER. Okay. How about Vietnam? So you are out of Cuba, out of Iran, but on to Vietnam. Okay. That is all right.

Have either one of you fellows been in the Cayman Islands?

Mr. HERDE. I have not.

Mr. MIDDLEMISS. No, sir.

Mr. ROHRABACHER. You guys must have been in the Cayman Islands.

Mr. DELAHUNT. Neither have I, Mr. Chairman, unfortunately.

Mr. ROHRABACHER. Now, let me note that I have been in the Cayman Islands, and I think something that is interesting in the Cayman Islands is that they have a thing called Ray Bay. Raise your hands in the audience if you have been to the Cayman Islands.

Mr. DELAHUNT. There are a lot of bankers out there, Mr. Chairman.

Mr. ROHRABACHER. A lot of bankers out there. So in the Cayman Islands, they have a thing called Ray Bay, and they have taught these vicious sting rays—I am a surfer, and I will tell you, if you step on a little sting ray, you are in big trouble, and I have stepped on a sting ray out surfing one time, and it is horrific. But these sting rays are beyond anything you could imagine. They are huge, like three and four feet across, and in the Cayman Islands, they have trained these rays to eat out of people's hands. You get into the water, and they come all around you, and they have taught these deadly creatures to eat right out of your hand and to cozy up to you.

My guess is that if they can do that with sting rays, they probably do that with those who are designed to regulate international financial institutions because somebody is not using their stinger, and obviously this has been a very interesting way to open the door.

I appreciate both of you testifying, and I will have to say that whoever briefed you, Mr. Herde, did a good job, and you did a good job, but even as professionally as they can brief you on how to say something specifically that does not create a liability—being a former journalist, I hear reasonable words of how to get around certain things. It is not you. I understand you are here representing your institution, and you did a fine job, but there were some questions that I believe were brought up by the way you answered certain things, "to the best of my personal knowledge, blah, blah," which indicates to me that there is probably someone very high up in the bank who knew everything and is still there.

Mr. HERDE. Sir, if I could take a moment to correct that.

Mr. ROHRABACHER. Sure. Absolutely.

Mr. HERDE. I would not want you to be left with the misimpression that those who were responsible were not treated appropriately and disciplined. The investigation found and allocated responsibility, and senior management acted on that. So everything that the investigation found was acted upon by management or by our regulators. I am not aware of any person who has escaped.

Mr. ROHRABACHER. "I am not aware" is a very good caveat, as I say. Ms. Ros-Lehtinen?

Ms. ROS-LEHTINEN. Thank you so much, Mr. Chairman, again.

Mr. Herde, your bank has stated that you now see the wisdom in not doing business with U.S.-sanctioned countries. I am interested in what the factors were that contributed to this earth-shaking decision and why it took so long. January is when you made the decision, January. Correct?

Mr. HERDE. I believe it was in November.

Ms. ROS-LEHTINEN. November. November——

Mr. HERDE [continuing]. Of last year.

Ms. ROS-LEHTINEN [continuing]. Of last year. How many months ago was that?

Mr. HERDE. That is about 6 months when the decision was formally finished.

Ms. ROS-LEHTINEN. Now, before that November date—we have this Congressional Research Service, and it has a timeline of the scandals, investigations, and violations involving UBS, and it is quite lengthy, and it goes page after page, and it is just surprising to me that it had taken so long. Here is the timeline that they had put out. UBS promised to cooperate with investigations into money laundering from Iran and Cuba. The National Association of Securities Dealers looking into UBS. A French investigation reported that Osama bin Laden had use of an account at UBS. All of these—I mean, it is just page after page. Serbian President Milosevic was reported to have profited. Here is another one, a Federal lawsuit.

It is just ongoing, and yet November, 6, 7 months ago, was when you finally put out your position statement. Here, a *60 Minutes* report named UBS as one of the banks holding Saddam Hussein's hidden assets. A bank spokesman described the charge as most unlikely.

So much was going on, and it is just page after page of so many activities. So what were the factors that contributed to your decision that it is not good business to do business with U.S.-sanctioned companies and what took you so long?

Mr. HERDE. Thank you, Congresswoman. I think, most importantly, we are quite proud of the fact that we are the first non-U.S. bank to take this step, and we do not think it took that long at all. In fact, no other bank, to our knowledge, has taken a similar step.

Second, as of today, everyone in the world except those in the United States and UBS are able to deal with Iran freely. There are not any sanctions outside of the United States on that country. We are wholly supportive of our global sanctions compliance program. We think it is the right step, and we think we took it for the appropriate reasons.

Ms. ROS-LEHTINEN. In April 2004 is when the Federal Reserve imposed a civil fine of $100 million. Is that correct? At 5/2004?

Mr. HERDE. Yes.

Ms. ROS-LEHTINEN. And then 6 months ago, you formed your position paper.

Thank you, Mr. Chairman.

Mr. ROHRABACHER. All right. Before we call the next set of witnesses, I saw some heads shaking yes or no out there, did Milosevic ever have a personal account with your bank?

Mr. HERDE. Milosevic. I have no knowledge.

Mr. ROHRABACHER. Well, there is another caveat. What about bin Laden? Did he have an account at your bank?

Mr. HERDE. I do not believe so.

Mr. ROHRABACHER. A caveat. Saddam Hussein; did he have an account at your bank?

Mr. HERDE. No, I do not think so.

Mr. ROHRABACHER. No, I do not think so, or I do not think so, no?

Mr. HERDE. I would be very happy to take these queries and answer them specifically.

Mr. ROHRABACHER. Okay. Now, let me ask you this, then. If we asked you those questions, can the answer get back within 2 weeks? Ileana has had a pretty rough time.

Ms. ROS-LEHTINEN. Thank you, Mr. Chair.

Mr. HERDE. My colleague advises me the answer is no to all three questions.

Mr. ROHRABACHER. No to all three questions. Of course, your colleague is not sworn in, but that is all right.

Mr. HERDE. That is true, but I am happy to——

Mr. ROHRABACHER. We will accept those. Again, I appreciate the fact that you are here. This has been a very illuminating hearing so far. We have got a second panel. You have done a good job by those people who are paying you. I want everybody out there to hear this. He has done a good job at representing his bank and his employers. That is not to say we have the same interests because we do not. We are here to represent the interests of the people of the United States of America, and we are trying to do a good job, too. But we can see that you are well intended, and you are doing a good job for those who are employing you, and we appreciate the good faith in having you here to answer these questions.

Ms. ROS-LEHTINEN. And I include that as well, Mr. Rohrabacher.

Mr. HERDE. Mr. Chairman, I would like to reiterate my thanks to you for inviting us to participate in this hearing, and I mean that in a genuine way. You have made clear a number of times that you have appreciated the good faith that the bank has extended, and it is our full intention to cooperate with all——

Mr. ROHRABACHER. Okay. Well, I am hoping that this set of hearings will open up a doorway to the world to start getting at some real international bad guys, some real evil people that are doing this throughout this globe and pilfering billions and billions of dollars that belong to the poor people of this world or even the regular people of this world. If you are going to be on our side in that, we do not care if anybody has made mistakes in the past. We are very happy to have your active support and cooperation in that effort. Mr. Middlemiss?

Ms. ROS-LEHTINEN. Mr. Chairman, if I could add, I hope that in the next set of hearings, we do not have to threaten anyone with any subpoenas to get them to be so cooperative, so I look forward to that.

Mr. ROHRABACHER. But in the next set of hearings, we are going to be investigating the Administration. I am just kidding.

Mr. DELAHUNT. I can assure you that will not happen. We will never investigate this Administration until I am sitting in that chair, and he is sitting over here.

Mr. Middlemiss, would you please convey my warm regards and best wishes to District Attorney Morgenthau?

Mr. MIDDLEMISS. That will be my pleasure.

Mr. ROHRABACHER. And thank you very much for your good work. Okay? Thank you very much. This panel is dismissed, and we have a second panel.

[Pause.]

Mr. ROHRABACHER. All right. We are back in session, the International Relations Committee, Subcommittee on Oversight and Investigations. We now have a panel, and for the record, we will be putting your entire bios in the record rather than have me read them right now.

We have with us Rodney Gallagher of Gaffney, Gallagher & Philip. We have Mr. Robb Evans of Robb Evans & Associates. We have with us John Moscow, who is a partner with Rosner Moscow & Napierala, and then Jonathan Winer, a partner of Alston & Bird.

So with that said, if you can make it 5 minutes and facilitate a discussion, that would be much appreciated. So, Mr. Gallagher, you may proceed.

Mr. GALLAGHER. Thank you, sir.

Mr. ROHRABACHER. And it would be very good to get the thing close to your mouth so that everybody in the hall can hear.

**STATEMENT OF MR. RODNEY M. GALLAGHER, OBE, PARTNER, GAFFNEY, GALLAGHER & PHILIP**

Mr. GALLAGHER. Thank you, Chairman. Thank you for the opportunity to be here today. In the interests of leaving room for my colleagues on the panel, I will, with your permission, merely pick out highlights of a written submission which I presented here today.

Let me speak first about the issue of corruption, which is a key feature for these hearing. I share the concerns that you expressed earlier, and, in parentheses, I will perhaps just comment that I was recently sent a copy of a report from the House of Commons Foreign Affairs Committee talking about the very same issue of corruption just 10 days ago. I am putting a figure of $150 billion a year on the cost of corruption in the context of the size of the problem that we all face.

I would like to make the point, particularly when we consider corruption, that essentially it is theft. We do not need to beat around the bush about what corruption is; it is stealing, and the only thing that distinguishes this from of stealing from any other is that it essentially requires two people, one to be corrupted and the other to corrupt.

Ms. ROS-LEHTINEN. And a nicer set of clothes.

Mr. GALLAGHER. Yes. And what that does, by way of a concept, is to make every act of corruption a conspiracy. It is a conspiracy between two people to steal, and it is nothing more complicated than that. But because it is a conspiracy, for the investigator, it is often rather more difficult to penetrate.

When we look at corruption, we need to recognize, in fairness to all concerned, that this is not merely a public sector problem; it is a private sector problem as well, and the only reason that we do not see so much of it in the private sector is that, in my experience, private sector corruption is something which is hastily swept under the carpet for fear by management that it may indicate to shareholders that they are not up to their jobs and that the share price might subsequently suffer. But we should not fool ourselves into thinking that corruption is not endemic in the private sector as it is in the public. But I will say that in the private sector, I have noticed that they are rather quicker to try to get the money back, whereas in the public sector, recovery of the money seems to be often less of a concern.

In the public sector, most of the inquiries we see into corruption have a straightforward political dimension. Generally speaking, it is a new government elected on a mandate to clean up which comes into power and attempts to examine circumstances surrounding corrupt practices by members of previous governments.

This level of corruption, which we see both in public and in private but perhaps more obviously demonstrated in the public, displays a network of corruption and relationships that are, generally speaking, complex. I defined corruption as always involving two people. Speaking from my firsthand experience of corruption cases that I have directly investigated, the network of corruption and the number of people involved almost always runs into double figures.

Corruption survives, in large part, because the benefits of corruption are spread about, and as a conspiracy, it is often a conspiracy which involves whole groups of people. It is not narrowly focused on particular individuals.

Our experience and success of prosecutions in this area are very limited, in part because of the complexity of the conspiracy but also because of a lack of a will to pursue them. I cited in my paper one of the most straightforward examples of corruption that I have come across in a long time, which was the Prime Minister of Granada caught on video accepting a briefcase allegedly containing half a million dollars and claiming in his defense that it was really only $15,000.

That might give rise to a certain amount of dry humor, but, of course, the fact of the matter is it remains an unprosecuted allegation, one which seems, to everyone concerned, to be entirely straightforward and direct, and yet the authorities in Granada have found it impossible to prosecute it. Well, I think we must draw our own conclusions as to why that is.

The issue of money laundering is something which the international community has widely recognized. It seems to be a hallmark of an issue that has been widely recognized, that there should be a UN convention that bounds it, but it would appear to me that the presence or absence of a UN convention has made little or no difference to the process. If we face up to the way in which we have dealt with the problem of corruption in the large countries, I think it is clear that we have so far done very little.

The Financial Action Task Force is a creature of the large countries, essentially the OECD (Organization for Economic Co-operation and Development) countries plus a few others, 30 odd of the largest countries in the world. We have attempted within the FATF (Financial Action Task Force on Money Laundering) framework to deal with the problem of corruption by requiring that any politically exposed person, as defined by FATF, or someone closely related to a politically exposed person, should, when opening a bank account, be subject to special requirements, and this might be a useful step in the right direction.

But on a careful reading of the FATF recommendation, it is drafted in terms of a foreign politically exposed person, and the implication of that in very simple terms is that if a politically exposed person from the United Kingdom came and opened a bank account in the United States, a red flag would go up, but if a Member of Congress went and opened a bank in the United States, no flag would go up.

It seems to me entirely inappropriate for that restriction of a foreign politically exposed person to remain, and it drives me to the view that the process is largely window dressing. Indeed, it seems intended to avoid the problem of foreign corruption flowing into the financial institutions of the large countries. Now, it does not prevent foreign corruption. It simply says that if foreign corruption is to exist, we do not want any of that money coming through accounts which you have opened in our country, speaking from an FATF country perspective.

As you well know, various of the international bodies have put in place programs related to good governance in which they strive hard at the World Bank and similar international institutions to prevent corruption in respect of projects which they finance, but often those international agencies are handling program money given to them by other countries, and, as such, they have to be sensitive to the political concerns of those countries.

It is quite clear to anyone who has looked at the way that aid flows are used as a tool of international relations and diplomacy to quickly appreciate that criteria in respect of good governance are often overlooked when wider donor country political interests are at stake.

It is with regret that I have to say that it appears that there are very few countries around the world that can claim a wholly ethical foreign policy, particularly in regard to the aid flows.

In respect of money laundering, we have, I think, to recognize the sad truth that the problem with money laundering originates in the larger countries and not in the smaller, offshore, financial services centers. Funds flow, for example, into the Cayman Islands or into one of our Pacific offshore centers through the major financial centers, and just to make the point to you that the role of the major countries is often at the point at which a placement is made of illegal funds, and where the funds are often transferred on to offshore centers, that is frequently at the lairing stage of the money laundering process. And, of course, by the time the illegal funds are into the financial system, in a sense, it is too late.

What we need to be focusing on is the prevention of illegal funds, illicit funds, funds that are the proceeds of crime and corruption, entering the banking system in the first place, and the fact is that the vast majority of funds originate in the developing countries.

That placement of funds takes the benefit of camouflage that exists in a large financial center where there are lots of large transactions going through, in a place like New York, and if we look, for example, at the case of Montesinos, the Peruvian head of intelligence, he put very large cash sums into the banking system in the United States and Europe and the Far East before they were routed into secret bank accounts in various offshore jurisdictions, including the Cayman Islands, Aruba, or Curacao, from when the money quite typically went back into other bank accounts in the United States and Europe.

Now, of course, the reason for that is quite obvious—if you actually want to access the money, the last thing you want to do is to be turning up in a place that has very few foreign visitors. You want to be able to access the money in an easy way in the sort of place that you are likely to visit, which, in Mr. Montesino's case, was more likely to be Miami than the Cayman Islands.

However, this process has certainly exposed many of the problems that exist in the offshore centers, and it appears to me that the key one in that regard is the inability of both the regulators and the owners, the managers of operations in the offshore centers, to engage in effective due diligence and to avoid effectively dirty business.

[The prepared statement of Mr. Gallagher follows:]

PREPARED STATEMENT OF MR. RODNEY M. GALLAGHER, OBE, PARTNER, GAFFNEY, GALLAGHER & PHILIP

My name is Rodney M Gallagher OBE. I am currently a partner in Gaffney, Gallagher & Philip of Miami, Florida.

Thank you for the opportunity to be here today.

Over the last fifteen years I have been an observer of the issues related to corruption, money laundering and terrorism financing, as viewed through the window of offshore financial services jurisdictions, mainly in the Caribbean Basin.

In my role as Financial Services Adviser to the British Government I had a hand in the establishment of mechanisms to deal with the problem of concealing the proceeds of serious crime. As sole Commissioner I examined corruption related to a public sector project in the British Virgin Islands and as Chief Investigator I am assisting currently the Commission of Inquiry related to fraud on a large public sector project in St Vincent & the Grenadines.

My work with the British Government involved me, first hand, in the investigation of a number of instances of the laundering of the proceeds of corruption and other serious crimes, including drugs trafficking, through offshore financial services jurisdictions, mainly in the Caribbean.

I am currently a partner together with Ross Gaffney and Paul Philip, both formerly with the FBI, in the firm of Gaffney, Gallagher & Philip of Miami, Florida. We undertake financial investigations, asset recovery and security work across the US and the Caribbean.

## CORRUPTION

Let me begin with a brief overview of corruption in both the public and the private sector.

It is curious that we use the word corruption to describe an act that may be much more straightforwardly described as "theft". It is only the ancillary aspects of the theft that give rise to the need to use the word corruption. And the most distinctive ancillary feature is the conspiracy that always underlies corruption. More than one criminal is always involved in corruption.

Corruption applies equally to the private sector as it does to the public sector; but the private sector is far less disposed to launch a public inquiry and we therefore see far less of the problem. And in the private sector the key issue is recovery of the money, rather than a criminal prosecution. The private sector is always concerned that the circumstances that give rise to corruption indicate weak or failed management systems, which might be view amongst the shareholders as systemic and likely to affect the share value. There are strong incentives therefore to conceal the crime. We often only see private sector corruption when the matter is the subject of a criminal prosecution.

In the public sector most inquiries in to corruption have a political dimension, usually a new government elected on a mandate to "clean up" an earlier, allegedly corrupt regime. But even in the public sector there are strong motives to conceal corruption, even when it is detected, as once again it may indicate weak systems.

Both the public and the private sector efforts to deal with corruption face the problem of the conspiracy that always underlies any corrupt act. The conspiracies are seldom simple, and the relationships that support them are usually complex. Contrary to the popular view, few instances of corruption involve direct payments between the person making the request for a benefit and the person who can grant the benefit, although such crude examples do occur.

For example, there were allegations a year or two ago relating to the payment by a Swiss based individual to the Prime Minister of Grenada of US$500,000 in cash, caught on the security video of the house in Switzerland. The Swiss based individual claimed that the payment was for the grant of an Honorary Ambassador position. The Prime Minister acknowledged receiving cash but claimed it was only US$15,000. Despite the relative simplicity of these allegations it proved almost impossible to bring criminal charges against either of the parties concerned.

Where more complex, indirect benefits are provided, often through the actions of an unrelated third party, it is even more difficult to establish a criminal case. Here in the US you need look no further than the Volker Report on the UN Oil for Food programme. Financial intermediaries, banks and family friends, all may act to obscure the flow of benefits, which may sometimes even be in kind, or in the form of a negative action. Often simply forgetting to do something can be a benefit.

Frequently the structures that support the corruption and launder the proceeds are controlled at the very highest level of government. In the Ukraine President Lazarenko not only received huge amounts of money from foreign and local ventures he established his own bank in Antigua to handle the money, working through a number of third parties in Switzerland and the USA. At the time few people in the banking community knew of his involvement and those who were acting on his behalf did so with all the power of the state behind them.

WHAT IS BEING DONE ABOUT THE PROBLEM?

The international community has recognised the problem. There is a UN Convention that seeks to address the issue.

On the laundering of the proceeds of corruption the Financial Action Task Force has led the way in raising concerns about role of politically exposed persons in the financial sector. But may not have gone far enough.

FATF only seeks to address the problem of "foreign" politically exposed person, not domestic ones. This means that a bank, or other financial institutions will only give special attention to a foreign person, asking the question, "are you a politically exposed person, or are you related to one". Such an approach that concentrates only on the foreign PEP, flies in the face of all commonsense and appears to be window-dressing by FATF.

Indeed the entire FATF approach is designed only to avoid the problem of the proceeds of corruption flowing in to financial institutions in FATF member countries, not to strike at the real causes of the problem.

Various Governments and international bodies such as the World Bank have incorporated in to their overseas aid programmes criteria related to "good governance". At the margin these efforts are effective in limiting or denying aid flows to some countries. But anyone who understands that aid flows are only a tool of international relations will quickly appreciate that criteria related to good governance will often be over-looked in the wider interests of the donor state. There are very few countries that can claim a wholly ethical foreign policy approach.

MONEY LAUNDERING

In considering money laundering in offshore jurisdictions it is necessary to understand that almost all the transactions involved originate in, or flowed through the financial sector of the major developed countries, New York, London, Tokyo and Frankfurt.

The role of the offshore sectors is largely at the layering stage of money laundering, placement having been done in a major financial market, where it is easier to conceal a large transaction.

For example, in the case of Montesinos, the Peruvian Head of Intelligence, vary large sums of cash were entered in to the banking system in the US, Europe and the Far East before being routed to secret bank accounts in the Cayman Isands, Aruba and Curacao and then back to accounts in the USA and Europe. All the primary banks saw Montesinos as the ideal private banking client, requiring discrete handling and putting the funds in the name of family members.

The exposure of the offshore centres is in their limited ability to distinguish good business from bad, risky business from safe business. And the worst cases demonstrate weakness at the heart of the supervisory structures in the advanced countries. The case of Bank of New York and its involvement with Russian organised crime and poor banking practices in Europe is an example.

It is common for major financial institutions to establish subsidiary operations in the offshore centres and to route transactions, subsequently shown to be illegal, through them. Look no further than Enron for an example.

Where offshore centres have shown their weakness is in licensing of offshore financial institutions without rigorous due diligence. In most instances where the regulatory process is weak it has attracted fraudsters and low-level money launderers. It is possible for fraudsters to corrupt the political and regulatory process in a small jurisdiction.

In Grenada First International Bank, run by Gilbert Ziegler, effectively took control of the licensing regime. The political and regulatory structures were corrupted and numerous inadequate offshore banks were established. Nearly all the banks were merely the vehicles for simple fraud schemes that impoverished small, North American savers. Most have now been closed.

Law enforcement has not been slow to use the banking sector in offshore jurisdictions in "sting" operations, working on the basis that money launderers would flock to an apparently dubious offshore bank. In Anguilla the US and the UK cooperated to establish and operate an offshore bank intended to service Colombian drug traffickers in a scheme called Operation Dinero. The bank played a key role in the subsequent arrest and imprisonment of leading cartel members. The operation is testimony to the need that criminal have for secure banking services but it demonstrated to law enforcement the necessity for the offshore bank to have a partner entity in the USA to facilitate cash entry and provide wider banking services.

Despite the efforts of FATF, IMF-World Bank and national regulatory regimes money laundering continues apace, displaced but not deterred. In part this is due to the failure of the interdiction regime directed at the drugs trade and the growth of other forms of serious crime. But it is also testimony to the inability of regulatory mechanisms to stem crime. Financial institutions often file SAR's as a means of buying insurance against some future problem not to contribute to the fight against serious crime.

Most Currency Transaction Reports in the USA go un-investigated. The same is true of the vast majority of Suspicious Activity Reports in other countries. An overload of information in the system is retained by the authorities largely on the basis that is might be useful to some criminal investigation at a future date. But of course it seldom is.

In general the anti-money laundering regime has made only a minor contribution to addressing the threat of serious crime. The real purpose of the anti-money laundering regime appears to be intended to make the tracing of the financial flows easier for the investigators once the crime itself has been solved.

There is the further difficulty that the repressive anti-money laundering structures try to swim against the tide of free markets, price and profit signals. There is no extra profit to be made by establishing a vigorous compliance regime in a financial institution. On the contrary there is only extra expense, both in direct business costs and the reduction of available business.

The burden of regulation related to money laundering has reached, in recent years, to a level where business will no longer support it. The Wolfsberg Group of mainly European banks has demonstrated this point in their negotiations on recent European and FATF money laundering initiatives. In the UK the Bankers Association recently lobbied successfully on issues related to record keeping. It is clear that the increased level of anti-money laundering regulation is having a minor impact on criminal enterprise but a disproportionate impact on legitimate business.

## FINANCING TERRORISM

In the Caribbean we have seen little evidence of a flow of funds to finance acts of terrorism, despite the almost comic efforts of the US Treasury Department in their rush to judgement on accounts in the Bahamas held by New York based, Afghan originating diamond merchants in 2002.

Indeed in Europe the primary mechanism for the financing of the life style of terrorist bombers and their associates is clearly the social welfare programmes run by the state, augmented by criminal activity. Even in the US the amount of money required to finance a terrorist in the preparatory stages of an attack is so small as to be certain to be able to pass "under the radar". But what we have seen is a jockeying for a place at the anti-terrorism table by those concerned with the regulation of financial institutions, offering products that are inappropriate to the task.

Where large sums of money do flow they are not directly destined for terrorists but are defined as flowing to those who may be involved in the support of terrorists, such as schools, religious charities, Islamic welfare and legal defence groups. This broadening of the definition of the financing of terrorism only seeks to establish the credentials of those who wish to participate in the battle with their weapons of financial regulation. What it fails to recognise is the intelligence that may be gleaned about how this supporting infrastructure is financed. Penetration, not elimination is required.

There is widespread evidence that all terrorist groups ultimately become involved in criminal acts of extortion, kidnap for ransom, fraud and bank robbery, in part to support themselves but also just because they can.

It is vital that the focus on terrorism finance does not become viewed as a specialist function in which Treasury officials alone are the gatekeepers. All aspects of law enforcement need to be involved. The issue of identifying, not denying, the financial resources of terrorists and their supporters, needs to be broadly based. And the intelligence capacity to follow these links needs to be extended. This will not be done through the financial regulatory mechanisms developed to tackle traditional money laundering.

## TRANSPARENCY

It is no surprise that both corruption and money laundering need discretion or better yet, absolute secrecy. The banking sector is synonymous with secrecy.

Many of the problems that are related to both corruption and money laundering have their origins in secrecy. Offshore financial services jurisdiction traditionally offered confidentiality as a central feature of their marketing.

Transparency may be a partial solution to these problems of corruption and money laundering. If all public affairs were conducted in a completely open forum the scope for corruption would be reduced. If the process of award of all public contracts was displayed on the website of the public body concerned it would be more difficult to sustain corrupt practices.

Business transactions are often confidential from those in the financial sector that might be handling only part of the transaction, for example a wire transfer, on the grounds of client confidentiality. Recent efforts to require information about the sender and the recipient on a wire transfer have met with protests from some parts of the financial community. Commercial transactions flowing through the banking sector are usually anonymous. These procedures create the conditions that support "layering" in the money laundering process.

Many commercial transactions are considered confidential because the parties concerned wish to obscure their pricing policies, or more often the level of their profit margin. More transparency and openness would encourage competition and lead to lower prices, not something most monopolists want to see.

INTERNATIONAL COOPERATION.

In a global economy the problems of corruption and money laundering are international problems, not limited to offshore financial centres but running through the entire financial system. And of course the same is true of terrorism financing.

We have seen a growing network of international agreements designed to extend international cooperation. They all usually require the authorities in one country to carry out certain acts on behalf of the authorities of another country. And the twin issues of how timely and how effectively are the rocks on which the cooperation will flounder.

In Europe we have moved to a system where law enforcement officers can have jurisdiction across national borders. This has come from the need to keep up with criminals who are not constrained by borders. This model may be the way forward in the future and would have great relevance in North America and the Caribbean in the fight against all forms of serious crime.

Thank you for your attention.

Mr. ROHRABACHER. Mr. Gallagher, let us move on from there, and we can come back to due diligence on their part and perhaps due diligence on the part of the law makers to establish standards in the first place.

Mr. GALLAGHER. Yes.

Mr. ROHRABACHER. Mr. Evans?

## STATEMENT OF MR. ROBB EVANS, PRINCIPAL, ROBB EVANS & ASSOCIATES

Mr. EVANS. Thank you, Mr. Chairman. I would like to take just a little different perspective and maybe take exception with my colleague, Mr. Gallagher, on a couple of points. I am a retired banker, and what I have been doing for most of the last 10 years is getting the money back, the money that has been stolen, the money that has been laundered, and trying to get it back to its rightful owners.

There are a couple of points that I think are worth making relative to your inquiry. This is completely off the subject of my prepared remarks, which I will just leave for what they are. First of all, I think when you are talking about terrorists' money and the other kinds of money laundering, you have to remember very clearly that the terrorist financing is small dollars. It is clean money going bad in small amounts as opposed to what you are talking about in sanctions, which is very large dollars. They are very different problems, and they are critical.

I would like to share with you two experiences from two different islands, but before I do that, I would just like to point out that there is an island that does more money laundering than any other, and that is Manhattan. The island that does most of the money laundering in the world is Manhattan, but I would like to talk about a couple of other——

Mr. ROHRABACHER. Those little beads and mirrors——

Mr. EVANS. What we do in my organization is we trace money, and we try and recover it for the victims of fraud, and we do it mostly on behalf of the United States Government. I want to share with you very briefly, just to try to straighten out maybe a little bit of reputational risk here, one batch of money that went to two different islands.

This is money that was stolen in California, and it was routed to the Cayman Islands. We traced the money to the Cayman Islands, and we did a good deal of work in terms of doing the forensic investigation work, and we went down to the Cayman Islands to try and recover the money, and we shared the information with the government there.

Here is what the government did. As soon as we showed up and shared them the evidence, the first thing they did is they started their own investigation of the bank in question, which was an active bank in the Cayman Islands. They confirmed our findings, and they ordered the bank closed and liquidated. After getting proper authority from their courts, they provided us with all of the bank documentation so that we could go onward tracing the money elsewhere around the world. They arrested and prosecuted the bank officers and the local launderers. We had a prosecution going in California. They sent two witnesses from the Cayman Government to help us in our case, and they gave us the money back for distribution to the victims.

Now, as part of our tracing of that money, we followed a large bloc to yet another island, and this island nation is about to get a major handout of United States aid. We tracked $8 million to Vanuatu. We went down to Vanuatu, just as we did in the Cayman Islands, to share the information we had, to show them the documentation. We went with a written introduction from the staff of the Board of Governors of the Federal Reserve.

The Vanuatu authorities refused to meet with us. They tried to confiscate the money, which was clearly documented as money stolen from consumers that needed to go back to consumers. They tried to confiscate the money for their national treasury. In spite of repeated requests to discuss and try and resolve the matter in some fashion, in some kind of asset-sharing program or anything else, they have completely refused to for years now.

The bank in question where the money went to in Vanuatu continues to operate. Its largest single deposit is this stolen money, at least as nearly as we can tell. The same back is under indictment in the United States for money laundering, and its executives are fugitives.

Now, there are two contrasts, and what I would suggest to this Subcommittee is that the fight against international money laundering goes on on many levels. There are little leaks, and there are big leaks. Please do not forget the little leaks. These are critically important, and in your position, you can do a good deal to stop it. By putting the pressure on these small jurisdictions to shape up and try and do the right thing rather than try and profit from it, you can turn that around.

Now, in the Cayman Islands, I know the Caymans have been lambasted pretty thoroughly here today, and my job is not to defend them at all, but they got the message years ago. They have been extremely cooperative in our recovery efforts, as have a number of the other former British colonies. Not true every place else. So I would urge your attention to some of these smaller jurisdictions because they are just as much of the problem as some of the major jurisdictions.

[The prepared statement of Mr. Evans follows:]

PREPARED STATEMENT OF MR. ROBB EVANS, PRINCIPAL, ROBB EVANS & ASSOCIATES

The hearing title, "Offshore Banking, Corruption and the War on Terrorism," provides a wide scope of issues that could be addressed. Testimony priority has been suggested regarding the role of international banks. I am privileged and pleased to respond to your request, but with your permission, will take some latitude with the subject matter.

For the past fifteen years, our organization has been tasked with the mission of recovering stolen money and returning it to innocent investors or consumers in numerous state and federal fraud actions. In almost all cases, we are appointed by a Federal District Court on the nomination of the Department of Justice, Federal Trade Commission, Securities and Exchange Commission, Commodity Futures Trading Commission or a state regulator or law enforcement agency.

My comments here and verbally are strictly my own and should not be attributed to any of the agencies or entities with which we are privileged to work.

Most of my colleagues in our organization are career bankers. We became focused on international asset recovery work when we were asked to be Trustee for the U.S. assets in the infamous BCCI case years ago. In spite of over a hundred recovery cases since then, we still tend to look at the world more from a bankers glassy-eyed perspective than from that of the law enforcement or legal community with which we work so closely. My comments today should be taken in that context.

You have specifically asked for comment regarding how international banks help US sanctioned countries get around those sanctions. Others on this panel are eminently more qualified to address that subject than am I. Let me just say that if the sanctions are unilateral, creative minds will find a way. Multilateral cooperation is the key. Unilateral action is fraught with problems and the opportunities for evasion are as many as there are situations. As a Federal Receiver, I have encountered substantial challenges in jurisdictions with strict bank secrecy laws. As a foreign litigant, my appointment by the US Court must be recognized in the foreign jurisdiction. Often, there are other challenges to the powers of a foreign litigant in international asset recovery actions. Even in circumstances where the US Court has ordered the return of misappropriated funds, or ordered the defendant to repatriate stolen funds, foreign courts may not recognize those orders in the absence of international treaties or cooperation agreements.

There is a multilateral treaty for cooperation in drug trafficking cases, the Vienna Convention, negotiated nearly 20 years ago, which has 170 signatories as of January 1, 2005.[1] There is no comparable multilateral treaty for cooperation in international fraud and asset recovery actions.

Please permit me to make a brief, arguably, slightly off topic observation on the subject on international cooperation. We need to continually look for multilateral opportunities to fight the war against the international criminals. A proposed law that is an excellent opportunity for such international cooperation is the US Safe Web Act that passed the Senate last week and will soon be before you. I strongly recommend it for your consideration. While this proposed legislation is designed to facilitate international cooperation in the area of internet fraud, it is an excellent example of the kind of multilateral cooperation needed today. You may consider it a stretch for me to raise the issue of this piece of proposed legislation in this venue today, but there is a close link between internet fraud and offshore banking, so, because of the timeliness of the issue, I thought I would mention it here.

Others on this panel have or will address the roles of the major multinational banks. I, on the other hand, would like to draw your attention to the issue of a regulatory climate that still exists in some smaller jurisdictions. In those several countries that have not adopted, or technically adopted but not vigorously enforced, the strict anti-money laundering standards of the major industrialized countries, led by

[1] The 1988 United Nations Convention Against Illicit Traffic in Narcotic Drugs and Psychotropic Substances, opened for signature December 20, 1988, entered into force November 11, 1990.

the United States, imposed on the financial community, a banking environment survives where bad players can still thrive and carry on business for the benefit of money launderers, drug dealers, terrorists and other blights on our international financial system.

Unfortunately, sometimes the enthusiasm of some international banks that are upstream correspondents for banks from weakly regulated environments may be muted either by inattention or opportunism. Some may take advantage of the higher standards that have been adopted by banks active in the United States since passage of the USA Patriot Act. As you know, the Patriot Act imposes duties on correspondent banks in the United States to take some responsibility for the activity in so called 'nested accounts' where smaller institutions flow their dollar transactions through the accounts of larger ones. When new higher standards become the norm, an opportunity arose for those with weaker standards to profit.

Most offshore banking centers with legitimate international banking business have, in recent years, vigorously improved their anti-money laundering efforts. If our experience is representative, many have proven eager to assist in recovering stolen money for return to the victims of fraud. In most instances, however, the Receiver must initiate a private lawsuit, which reduces the amounts available for victim restitution.

But there remain recalcitrant jurisdictions who may pay lip service to anti-money laundering programs to the extent necessary to avoid black listing but whose real priority is obviously to protect indigenous institutions whose major role is to provide vehicles for hiding money from lawful authorities and rightful owners.

One of the Federal Trade Commission cases (FTC v. J.K. Publications)[2] my firm is handling has been cited often as a money laundering case study to illustrate that dark craft. I attach a graph my colleagues produced as a byproduct of our tracing investigation to illustrate just how it worked in that instance. This case and this graph have been used before to make various points about different aspects of money laundering.

I would like to use this case today to illustrate the different reactions by two different governments when confronted with evidence that stolen money was being laundered through one of their local banks.

In the Cayman Islands, we initiated a civil recovery action and presented the facts we developed in our case in California that documented the role of the Cayman bank in laundering the funds by the American fraudster. The Cayman authorities:

- Immediately investigated the bank, confirmed our findings and ordered the bank closed and liquidated.
- With proper court authority, promptly provided us with bank documentation to assist in the onward tracing of funds.
- Arrested and prosecuted bank officers and local launderers.
- Provided witnesses from the Cayman government in support of our U.S. case. Earlier this month my colleagues were in the Cayman Islands testifying in support of criminal prosecutions undertaken there.
- The money was returned to the U.S. Receiver for victim restitution.

Contrast that with the cooperation in one of the onward destinations of some of the money, the South Pacific island nation of Vanuatu where one of their banks, at the behest of the now defunct bank in the Cayman Islands, was sheltering a large block of the stolen money.

- After federal court agents traveled to Vanuatu with written introductions from the Federal Reserve and extensive documentation regarding the matter, the government and banking regulatory officials refused to meet or look at the offered documentation.
- The government tried to confiscate the money for their national treasury.
- Repeated requests to meet and discuss the matter continue to be ignored, years later.
- The bank continues to operate in spite of two of its officers being indicted for money laundering in another multi-million dollar fraud case in Memphis, Tennessee.[3] One defendant, Robert Murray Bohn, the President and CEO, was convicted of a RICO conspiracy and money laundering on October 25, 2005. The Bank's former Chairman, Thomas Montgomery Bayer, remains

[2] Federal Trade Commission v. J.K. Publications, et al., Case No. 99–00044 ABC (AJWX), (C.D. Cal.)

[3] USA v. Moss, et al, Case No. 2:02-cr-20165 BBD–ALL, (W.D. Tenn., Memphis)

under indictment. In the Memphis case, the US Attorney's Office and the Justice Department are seeking the forfeiture of approximately $14 million, representing a portion of the funds that were laundered by European Bank Limited through its correspondent bank account.

- In the JK Publications case, which is still pending in Vanuatu, the stolen funds, now in excess of $8 million, appear to be the bank's largest deposit.

Legitimate offshore international centers, such as the Cayman Islands, now have robust anti-money laundering programs and cooperate fully to recover illegal funds that find their way into their jurisdictions. Fringe financial centers have a more spotty record.

What should be of particular interest to this committee is that some of those same fringe centers on one hand frustrate U.S. policy, aiding and abetting the fleecing of U.S. consumers, and, on the other hand, apply for U.S. funding under various grant programs.

On the 2nd of this month, the Millennium Challenge Corporation, funded by U.S. tax dollars, signed a five year $65.69 million compact with Vanuatu. I have been to Vanuatu and I know that there are significant needs. But when a government repeatedly thumbs its nose at American courts and regulators and refuses even to meet and discuss if or how to return money undisputedly stolen from American citizens, is that country a proper priority for such aid?

I suggest that before such grants are given, or, in the case of Vanuatu, funded, countries with offshore financial centers should have their level of cooperation in the war against money laundering and international crime reviewed. Congress should insist that the funding of grants should be denied or deferred for those countries thwarting the efforts of the international regulatory and law enforcement community to curtail terrorist financing, money laundering or recovery of proceeds of fraud.

I particularly wish to emphasize the importance of encouraging cooperation in international fraud recovery. It is not enough for a jurisdiction to say they now bar black money if they do not facilitate the recovery of money stashed earlier.

Again, my thanks for giving me the opportunity to vent my frustration and point out a topic I think is worthy of your consideration. It will be a privilege to be of any assistance to the sub-committee in any way possible.

## Analysis of offshore activity originating from Receivership Defendants' funds

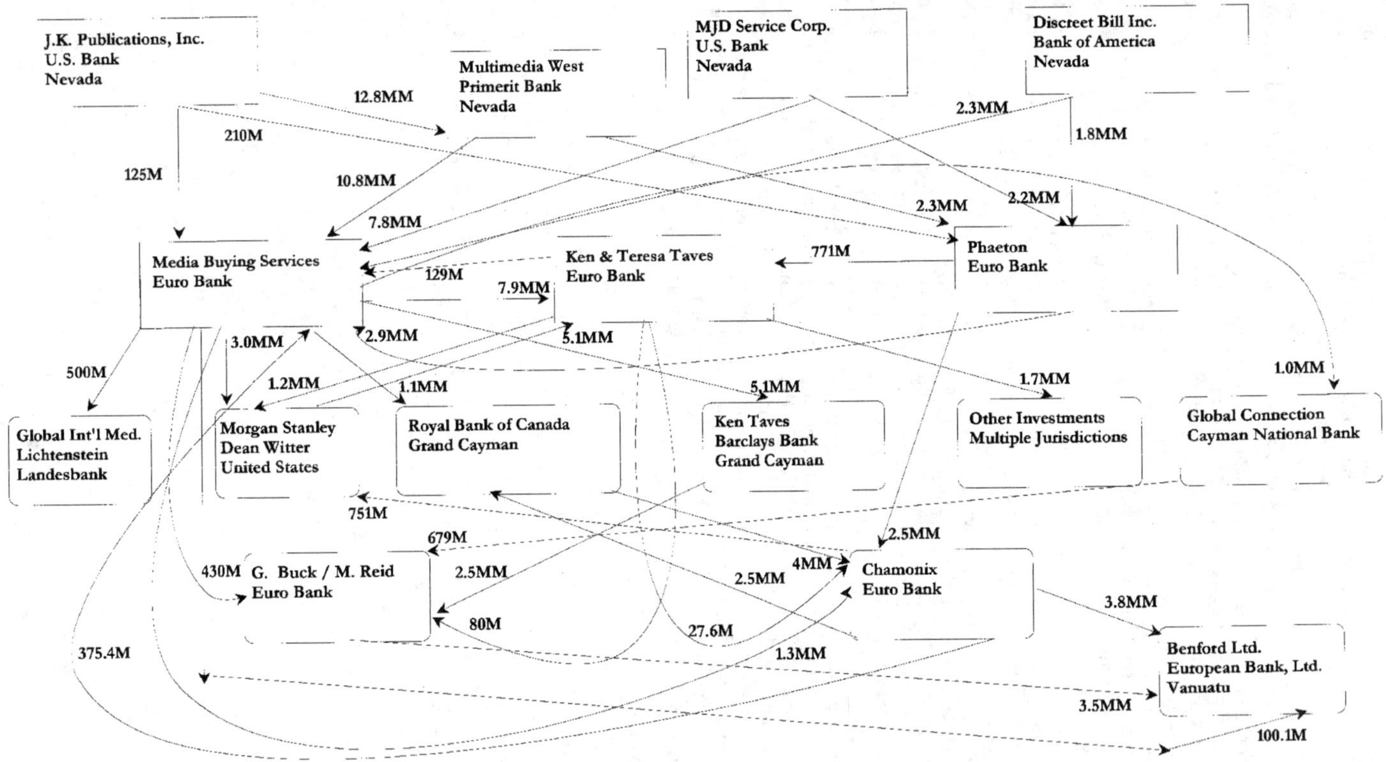

Mr. ROHRABACHER. Thank you very much, Mr. Evans. That was very good, off-the-cuff testimony.

Mr. EVANS. Could I just add one more thing, Mr. Chairman?

Mr. ROHRABACHER. Go right ahead.

Mr. EVANS. You showed some interest in the situation with Vietnam.

Mr. ROHRABACHER. Yes.

Mr. EVANS. In California, we have recently—as a matter of fact, literally tomorrow, we will finish the liquidation of a Vietnamese-oriented, money-transmittal company. Just for your information, and I do not know how analogous this is to the New York situation, but it was a similar situation where the remitters were not playing by the rules. They were not keeping the records. They were not doing the due diligence, and for this, among other things, their company was seized, they were shut down, and they are being prosecuted. I would point out to you that underlying that transaction is mostly small remittances from immigrants back to their families, not really criminal proceeds.

Mr. ROHRABACHER. Right. And, of course, if the bank would have probably paid off the dictatorship that now controls Vietnam, there might not have been the shutdown at all.

Mr. EVANS. Well, these are all folks just trying to feed their families.

Mr. ROHRABACHER. Except not the bank trying to feed the families; the bank trying to exploit the families.

Mr. EVANS. No. This is not going through the banks; this is going through money remitters.

Mr. ROHRABACHER. It is going through who now?

Mr. EVANS. Through these money-transmittal houses that were not operating legally.

Mr. ROHRABACHER. I see. All right. Thank you very much, Mr. Evans.

Mr. Moscow, if you could, again, try to compress it.

Mr. MOSCOW. I will do that.

## STATEMENT OF JOHN MOSCOW, ESQ., PARTNER, ROSNER MOSCOW & NAPIERALA, LLP

Mr. MOSCOW. Mr. Chairman, Members of the Committee, thank you. Having heard the discussion this afternoon, the question I want to address is, how can the situation be alleviated? That was the question that was posed. I do not think it is a pie-in-the-sky solution to suggest that we focus on the question of what kinds of secrecy are proper in transmitting money because it is all one world economic system now, and if you can hide the information on who is moving money, then that person is exempt from responsibility for their actions, does not have to pay taxes on it, and can use it in many improper ways.

So the three kinds of secrecy: Everybody wants secrecy from their neighbors. They want their bank affairs to be secret. The problems arise when you have laws which keep the information secret from law enforcement and from the courts. Whether it is divorce courts or criminal courts, it does not matter. And then, of course, you get total catastrophe when you have banks where the information is kept from the bank regulators because there the depositors' money will end up in the hands of the owners, and the banks will have collapsed.

But focusing on the law enforcement problem, many countries take the view that they cannot afford to have law enforcement learn about financial affairs because they do not trust them, they will be misused, or something like that. That is the problem. We cannot say that some countries are so badly governed that we are going to let them use secrecy as an excuse for people to commit crimes elsewhere in the world and hide, and that is really what it comes down to.

There are countries where they have changed the game, where the people who want to launder money have changed the way they do it. It is not bank secrecy anymore; it may be corporate secrecy. They will tell you what the bank accounts are, but they will not tell you who is doing it because it is an anonymous corporation. If it is not a corporation, it will be a trust. The amount of money in trusts now is beyond comprehension.

It is the case that financial institutions accept deposits from trust companies where they know the trust company, but the trust company may be in a jurisdiction where they do not necessarily know the beneficial owners of the trusts. There are trusts out there now, a lot of them, which seem to be trusts on the face of it, but if you look, you will not find out who the beneficial owners are because there may be somebody who has the option in the future of changing the identity of the beneficial owner. To say that you know your customer when there is somebody who can change the identity of the beneficial owner five levels down—this is very sophisticated stuff, but a lot of money that is being handled by people who want to break the law is going through that sort of channel.

Now, I do disagree with Mr. Gallagher about one point. He was talking about trying to stop illegal money entering the system. There are two kinds of money laundering we have to focus on. One is the cash that is generated by narcotics and other businesses, and the other, far more complicated and maybe too hard to deal with, are the stolen funds that come from the plutocrats, the people running the countries, where the money leaves as wire transfers. When the natural resources of Russia were being sold to companies, they were being paid for by wire transfers. Money was wired to New York, and then the banks that had wired the money would ask for currency, which would be shipped back to Russia.

When I was looking at that, I thought they were laundering money, but I was wrong. The money laundering had already been accomplished by the wire transfers. They were shipping the hundreds back to a country where people wanted to be able to put their hands on what they owned, cash.

So now we have money laundering both by wire and in currency, and what Rodney said was absolutely right for the currency part, but when the crimes that take place involve the sale and misuse of assets in sufficient quantity, it starts off as a wire transfer, and the job of a prosecutor, an investigator, an asset recoverer, is just that more complicated and, to a certain extent, that much more simple.

To conclude, what we need to do to clean up the system is to insist that every country and every financial institution, bank, brokerage firm, or otherwise, maintain honest records about the transfer of funds and there be a legal mechanism whereby people interested in prosecuting crimes involving those funds be allowed to get access to it, and if this means for some countries that they have to strengthen the integrity of their legal systems and of the people doing the investigations, that is a burden where perhaps the United States can help them, but it certainly is an easier way to approach this than any other. Thank you.

[The prepared statement of Mr. Moscow follows:]

PREPARED STATEMENT OF JOHN MOSCOW, ESQ., PARTNER, ROSNER MOSCOW & NAPIERALA, LLP

My name is John W. Moscow. I am a partner in the New York City law firm of Rosner Moscow & Napierala. From August 1972 through December 2004 I served as an assistant district attorney—a prosecutor—in the New York County District Attorney's Office, starting with Frank S. Hogan and continuing for the past thirty years with Robert M. Morgenthau. Over the past twenty five years I personally prosecuted and supervised the prosecution of sophisticated economic crimes involving large and small scale international theft, fraud, and, of necessity, money laundering.

I deeply appreciate the Committee's invitation to appear here this afternoon to discuss the role of off-shore banks in aiding capital flight, money laundering and other illegal activities including the possible support of terrorism, and in discussing how international banks help countries subject to sanctions by the United States get around the sanctions imposed by the United States. I appreciate the opportunity to clarify my own thoughts on what money laundering is, both as a defined crime, and more importantly, and as process, what if anything should be done about it, and what if anything can be done about it

The issues which you raise go directly to the heart of the operation of the world's financial system in which all countries of the world have interests, sometimes conflicting interests. Money is power. The ability to move money without detection is the ability to exercise power without being held accountable for the uses to which the money is put. Between the funding of narcotics dealers, the protection of plutocrats destroying the economies of their home countries to put money aside for themselves, their families, and friends, the destruction of the tax bases of the industrialized nations, the use of foreign funds to swing elections and the horrible corrosive consequences to the idea of government legitimacy, the process of money laundering through financial institutions must be of concern to us all.

In talking about money laundering I bring to bear a perspective which is uniquely my own, with a background that not everyone here shares. I am not a banker, nor a bank regulator. I do not work for a Fortune 500 company, a trade association or an international law firm.

Rather I was an assistant district attorney in Manhattan—New York County, to use its official name—who spent many years charged with prosecuting those crimes and offenses committed in the 22 square miles of the County, or within the county's jurisdiction as defined; a very different matter indeed, as you will hear.

Starting in 1977 I prosecuted economic crimes, sophisticated and simple, which make up the criminal side of the white-collar world in Manhattan. I have dealt with securities frauds, frauds against government agencies, tax shelter frauds, and corruption cases. Starting in 1989 I examined or prosecuted the Bank of Credit and Commerce, International (BCCI), certain aspects of the collapse of the Venezuelan banking system, events at the Bank of New York and a number of substantial international securities frauds involving victims from around the world. My views are those of someone who has sought to gather evidence of financial crimes, and had that evidence withheld.

In speaking with you I would like to thank two men who have greatly influenced my thinking in this area. One is my boss, Robert M. Morgenthau, the District Attorney of New York County, who has led the fight against money laundering for the past 35 years. The other is Dr. Barry Rider, the one-time Director of the Institute for Advanced Legal Studies in London, and the moving force behind the Cambridge Symposium on Economic Crime. He has contributed greatly to my understanding of the situation, but who is not to be held accountable for what I say. My views are my own, and I speak only for myself.

First some definitions are in order. There are statutes in various jurisdictions making "money laundering", as various defined in different jurisdictions, a crime.

And in fact money laundering should be a crime. But it is more important to consider what money laundering really is, a process of concealment, lest we get caught up in trivializing definitions.[1]

"Money laundering" it is a process for the concealment of evidence, in which a person seeks to evade responsibility for the ownership, origin or the use of funds. A person who seeks to launder funds wants to able to achieve results without having to accept responsibility for such results or the means used the achieve them. He wants the benefits of ownership, without any of its liabilities. And those benefits can be achieved by laundering money. Money can be laundered in a variety of ways—smuggling currency, unwritten underground banking transactions, use of banks in jurisdictions with bank secrecy, or corporate secrecy, or an inappropriate use of trusts, among other means.

For you to follow my conclusions as to where we are and where we are going to be in a few years a little background is in order.

The fight against money laundering was initially started by Robert M. Morgenthau in the mid-1960s, when he, as United States Attorney for the Southern District of New York, was thwarted in gathering evidence from Swiss Banks and certain subsidiaries of American banks about Unites States securities fraud and United States Army black marketeering. That fight gathered strength with the war against drugs, and both Congress and the American bank regulators adopted the cause. Congress in 1986 passed an anti-money laundering law which has dramatically changed the face of American law enforcement, even though it did not make illegal the transfer of funds from such national leaders as Marcos, Salinas, Mobutu, Suharto, Abacha or Pinochet.[2]

Bank regulators have, over the past nineteen years, adopted the anti-money laundering cause as their own. Entire new bureaucracies have been created within the ranks of the regulators and the regulated to deal with the problem; this aspect of the war against drugs looks as though it has become an employment tool.[3] With the passage of the USA PATRIOT Act in October 2001 those tendencies were re-enforced by adding anti-terrorism to the tasks anti-money laundering personnel are supposed to undertake.

Entire new regulatory entities—the Financial Action Task Force, Financial Stability Forum, and now even groups from OECD—have sprung up to measure compliance with anti-money laundering suggestions, best practices or regulations. And, while that has been going on, there has been a serious change in emphasis over time from fighting the narcotics trade to collecting taxes to fighting terrorism.

When Bob Morgenthau started to fight bank secrecy statutes, many countries took the view that it was not their place to enforce the tax laws of another country. They wanted to have bank secrecy in place so that they could profit by assisting people with commission of "fiscal" offenses' or tax fraud. It appears that much of the social acceptance underlying this was based on the post-World-War II tax regime in England (and much of Europe) under which Labor governments set levels of taxation of income and estates so high that much of society was quite willing to violate the law, or at least was willing to support ostensible lawful excuses for tax evasion.

Great Britain, after World War II, became an intellectual centre of bank secrecy practices, designed by the upper classes to protect their family wealth from confiscatory taxes; the intellectual heritage of that tradition continues today, even though the facts have changed enormously since then. Crown colonies and Crown dependencies such as Jersey, Guernsey, Isle of Man, Gibraltar, and Cayman started as offshore financial jurisdictions to assist UK residents. But the tradition of asking no questions left those money centers wide open to abuse by others than British aristocrats seeking to preserve their inherited wealth.

Narcotics dealers, and the money launderers they employed starting in the 1970s, gleefully exploited the bank secrecy practices adopted to protect tax evaders. The money-launderers' use of bank secrecy statutes became the stuff of legend, and

---

[1] The differences in definitions may make extradition from nation to another for international money laundering far more complex than it should be.

[2] The federal anti-money laundering covers almost all local crime, such as securities fraud, bankruptcy fraud, and harboring an illegal alien. The penalties for money-laundering, however, are draconian, and, taken with the federal guidelines, have given federal prosecutors far more power, individually, than they have ever had, and have incidentally given the cause of fighting money-laundering a very bad name.

[3] There are huge numbers of compliance personnel, analysts, computer software specialists and attorneys and others at the major money center banks charged with fighting money laundering and terrorism. They run name checks through data banks, and attempt to analyze transactions. But hey do not at many institutions either know or speak to the customers to ascertain what a transaction represents.

fraudsters seeking to hide money other than tax money and narcotics proceeds started to use the same techniques.

By the mid 1990s the European Union and the United States were beginning to attack tax havens bitterly. For the governments it was and still is, a matter of survival. As transnational corporations manage their affairs to minimize taxes paid, they deprive all governments of tax revenue. In Europe and the United States the middle classes have been following their lead. For those of us who believe in the rule of law, depriving democratic governments of revenue by manipulating the laws of offshore havens is exceptionally bad government, as I discuss below.

For a few years in the 1990s it appeared that there would be constant pressure on the offshore jurisdictions to clean up their act. Some jurisdictions have done so, many more wish to create the appearance, but not the reality of having done so, and some are overtly willing to accept dirty money as a source of business. The certifications by international bodies that nations were "cooperative" may not, in the long run, turn out to be more than pious wishes.

During the decades since the fight for and passage of the Bank Secrecy Act of 1970, the people who launder money for a living have not been passive. They have stayed well ahead of law enforcement in devising new techniques for separating ownership of money and other assets from the responsibilities for that ownership and for the use of the power that ownership bestows. And some of them work at banks, some of them are accountants and some of them are attorneys. As law enforcement has chased old stereotypes, the professional launderers have adjusted to changing conditions.

The old picture of a Colombian drug dealer driving into a bank with valises filled with currency is not now quite accurate. Rather than walk into a U.S. bank with lots of ash, which now would raise questions, smugglers transport most narco-dollars out of the United States for deposit in jurisdictions in which there are no forms to fill out,[4] but other people too work to launder money.

Elegant lawyers, registered lobbyists, and public relations firms all represent the money laundering industry's efforts, even though the industry is still largely based on drug selling in the streets. "Campaign contributions," were in recent years made by groups such as the Texas Bankers Association, to get government to take "a more balanced view" of the anti-money-laundering fight. (When a lobbyist for the American Bankers Association opined, publicly, that a particular bill would not harm the banking industry, he was privately but severely chastised by a senator who had accepted money from the lobbyists for Antigua, and told he must in the future oppose all bills strengthening the fight against narcotics money-laundering, even if the bankers were not adversely affected.)

Many years ago Winston Churchill wrote that he could not engage to remain neutral as between the fire brigade and the fire; that senator wanted the ABA to actually hinder the firemen. I wonder why. Some have suggested it is because the Senator has a visceral distaste for regulation. All that is clear is that his ideology or his financial self-interest (in the campaign contributions) caused him to ignore the reality of what he was doing.

When the narcotics lobby and the anti-tax lobby[5] were fighting together against anti-money laundering legislation and regulation, the Board of Governors of the Federal Reserve System proposed new " KYC" regulations, which, after a fight, resulted in their being withdrawn. Individual rights and consumer privacy were advanced as the reasons for the KYC debacle, but the banks use the information sought for their internal commercial use as we speak.

It must be conceded that the KYC regulations, as proposed, were out of date. By the mid 1990s it was no longer appropriate for the full weight of the anti-money laundering fight to be born solely by banks, when financial service providers are all equally available for abuse by the criminals. Merrill Lynch is not a bank for regulatory purposes, and was not been subject to KYC regulation until the USA PATRIOT Act was passed, even though it had, for a while, more money on deposit in its money market accounts than did any bank in the USA.

---

[4] The Colombians have excess dollars; the Russians, for example, want U.S. dollars. It appears that the two groups are working together to launder money outside regular channels for their mutual benefit. I note that the Russians are now seriously involved in the heroin trade with Europe, and suggest, on scanty evidence, that the "businessmen" are far ahead of the regulators and the policemen in this area.

[5] Tax shelters, if valid, do not need to be secret.

The securities markets likewise are woefully wide open to money-laundering, but until the PATRIOT Act was passed the industry and the SEC took the view that there was no money laundering in the markets.[6]

The insurance industry is also wide open to abuse; there is little perceptible regulation at all in the insurance field. Recent cases show, however, that insurance companies can easily be used by launderers to cleanse their money at reasonably low cost.

The trust industry has been exceptionally creative, coming up with legal-sounding "trusts" which probably are not lawful in the United States, by which the beneficial ownership of the trust is concealed. So too is the actual control of trust assets. We are seeing trusts with "nominee beneficial owners," which may sound good if you say it quickly, but means nothing but "I won't tell you who the owner is" when analyzed.

In this context we have varying forces at work.

The money-laundering lobby seeks to end all efforts to combat money laundering, sometimes under the guise of privacy, sometimes in an anti-tax mode. The bureaucrats seek to expand their own regulatory anti-money laundering empire. A large pool of people is now engaged, at great effort and expense, to combat money laundering by ticking boxes on forms to see if transactions are "suspicious, " largely because the costs of investigating transactions is so large.[7]

The Executive Branch reflects several different aspects of this complex situation. Ideologically the administration is opposed to drug dealers and bureaucrats. The Bush designees in the Department of Justice had a far more sophisticated view of money laundering than those in the Clinton administration. (I note that under Clinton efforts to seize currency being exported from the USA were cut way back, even though Justice and Customs knew that we had effectively closed the banking system to dollar deposits, and that the implication was that narcotics dollars had to be exported.)

In addition there is pressure from the United States Senate to combat money laundering effectively. Senator Carl Levin of Michigan, on the Government Operations Committee, and similarly minded colleagues have been seeking to have the financial services community assist in the fight against money-laundering, and terrorism; since September 11, 2001 they have gotten a great deal of help. But the help is from people in compliance and regulation; it needs to be the CEOs, the COOs, and the full operational team of each institution.

The problem which has arisen is that as technology changes, the money-transmission part of banking has become exceedingly vulnerable to customer abuse. The entire problem faced by the Bank of New York ("BNY") in 1997–98 was due to a wonderful set of technological advances the Bank had implemented, without thought as to the possibility of their misuse.

Simply put, BNY allowed customers unfettered access to its computers to receive and transmit wire instructions from anywhere the customer's computer could be reached by telephone. That, today, is anywhere. We could call it Banking at Home. The use, at the Bank of New York, was restricted to whomever the customer wanted to allow in-itself an invitation to disaster. The technology permitted each customer to engage in correspondent banking with unlicensed correspondents. And following the attacks on the Unites States on September 11, 2001, Congress dealt with that in the USA PATRIOT Act, but the money launderers have changed their tactics, and are using corporate secrecy jurisdictions and trusts to hide the identity of the principals for whom they act.[8]

In the future, what should we do? It is something this Committee is extremely well suited for. We should work together to establish the rule of law, worldwide. For the reasons I describe below we should join to abolish bank secrecy laws and practices, including corporate secrecy laws and abusive trusts, insofar as they keep evidence from prosecutors and courts. We should fight to abolish corporate secrecy, and refuse to deal with anonymous corporations. We should bar anonymous trusts through which billions of dollars a year pass without the beneficial owners' identities being known, much less being published.

---

[6] The work of Neil Jeans, then at the National Crime Squad of England and Wales, demonstrates how easy it is to use the markets to launder money; my own cases tend to support his conclusions.

[7] The size of the work-force necessary to police transactions has been forcing all but the largest banks out of the business of transmitting dollars, increasing the concentration of business in few hands.

[8] The inclusion in the European Community of nations like Cyprus, with a long history of permitting bank and corporate secrecy, makes European tracing of funds far more difficult than it was.

We should make sure that we know or if necessary can learn which people are responsible for each amount of money going through financial institutions. Keep in mind that prosecutors and counter-terrorism agents need evidence to proceed. They need real evidence, not tick marks in boxes on forms. An agent who asks for the name of the person who authorized a transfer of money does not want to be told that the transfer was authorized by a British Virgin Islands company established in Tortola by a Mexico City law firm at the request of a Swiss lawyer who said that his unnamed client was highly valued. The question was "who authorized the transfer?" The answer should be a name.

An example of the wrong sort of behavior can be found (easily) in Cayman, when, some years ago the Irish authorities were seeking evidence about payments to a Prime Minister of Ireland from the Ansbacher bank. Initially the Cayman court told the Irish authorities to "Get Lost," citing bank secrecy. A few years later Ansbacher went into Court, because it was under pressure in Ireland to release the evidence. Cayman's Chief Judge, Anthony Smellie, authorized the bank to release the information as to the flow of funds, but barred the bank from identifying the parties directing the transfers, receiving the money, or controlling the accounts. With that information withheld, the information released was of no value; Cayman continued to keep evidence from the courts and legislature of Ireland, whose processes would have been compromised by bribes, on the intellectually trivial argument that Cayman bank secrecy is more important.

That Cayman view favored criminals. It was not, however, irrational for Cayman to value its secrecy more than Irish integrity, so long as they accept a view of their role in the world as economic parasites, selling their sovereignty for cash to everyone who wants secrecy from courts of law for his business dealings. If they choose to change that view, and they ay, they have to change their behavior.

It is apparent from my perspective that the world economy has become a global marketplace, in which some countries are better able to participate than others.[9] That is because honest markets demand the rule of law, and some nations either can not or do not choose to be bound by laws. Money laundering, as I define it, is the concealment of evidence from courts of law as to the ownership, origin, or use of funds to evade responsibility for the use.

*The Role of Rule of Law in the Business World*

The April 18, 1998 edition of the Financial Times asserted editorially that

> At the national level the emerging global standard consists of liberal trade and open financial markets. It demands a high quality of regulation, and independent legal processes, to protect private property and handle bankruptcy. It calls for non-corrupt government. Within this framework prosperity is generated by free competition among profit-seeking companies.

Whether we will ever obtain the utopia of prosperity through free competition among profit seeking companies is something which time will tell. Experience teaches me, however, that high quality regulation, independent legal processes, including independent prosecutors, honest judges, and non-corrupt government are necessary to avoid disaster, even if they can not generate prosperity. What The Financial Times proposed, and what appears to me beneficial, is establishing the rule of law in the worldwide economy. That requires a certain amount of change.

Simply put, in the twenty-odd years since the Reagan-Thatcher era started there has been a revolution in the roles of government and business. Power shifted at an incredible pace from government to business, especially with the end of the Cold War and the diminished need for "National Security" to be pre-eminent. The needs of international business for government are relatively few; they are concerned with everyone getting a level playing field. (I do not suggest that any business wants a level playing field; they each want the edge over their competitors. Collectively that means the field should be level.)

With the arrival of international nihilistic terrorism, such as the attacks on the World Trade Center, however, there are countervailing pressures leading to even stronger anti-money laundering pressures.

Some of the new pressures, such as the USA PATRIOT Act, are having a serious impact on world banking, by, for example, requiring all correspondent banks in the United States to appoint an agent for the service of legal process. It can have that impact and still not affect Bank of New York sorts of money laundering, however. We do not need so much in the way of detailed regulation as wholehearted and honest record keeping, with no place for people to hide from law enforcement the actions they have taken. But that is not the direction in which we are going. We are getting more and more formalistic in our anti-money laundering regulation, without really getting serious about combating the laundering of money.

I am reminded of an old definition-that a fanatic is a person who, having lost sight of his objective, redoubles his efforts. It appears to me that the bank regulators have lost sight of why it was important for a bank to know its own customer—"KYC" in the regulatory parlance. It is important so that we know who to hold accountable if money is misused, whether to violate securities laws, generate wealth for narcotics dealers, or pay for the care and training of terrorists. Honest, accurate, complete records which can be accessed when necessary by law enforcement is what is needed. Financial institutions may not have the capacity to know everything about their customers, but it is not great burden to require them to maintain hones, complete and comprehensive records of dealings with other people's money. An institution simply has to keep records of the identity of the person who moved money through it.

Banks, brokerage firms and insurance companies and their customers are, or own companies which create value in the world. They are creatures of law, and, by and large, with inevitable exceptions, they try to follow the laws of the countries in which they do business. Banks live by, and rely on, the rule of law in every commercial transaction in which they engage. The honest businesses with which banks deal rely on it as well. But there are other business interests in the world than those which are honest.

It is worth locking at a few patterns involving money laundering.

Being successful in the global economy makes a businessman the target of thieves—of people who want to undercut established manufacturers' prices without incurring their costs. Under the law they can not do this, so they break the law. (I focus on business here, because that is where the money is). Whether the issue is patent, or trademark or copyright, a manufacturer who does not pay royalties can easily undersell one who does.[10]

NECESSARY LEGAL EVIDENCE

The rule of law involves the use of legal mechanisms to defend property rights. And the clearest way I know to accomplish that end—to protect production and creation of goods—is to put in jail the people who steal property and to seize or forfeit the proceeds of their crimes. Such actions require the use of courts, and, to be successful in court, the gathering of valid, accurate evidence. Having said that, let me add that collecting such evidence is a daunting task, requiring intensive investigation into the source of goods, and requiring a more complicated, if less manpower-intensive investigation to trace the proceeds of the crime.

Identifying the originators of contraband goods by tracing goods backward starts at the level where the goods are sold. (The goods could be drugs, or stolen goods, or counterfeit goods, it does not matter. I refer to them all as contraband.) One can, theoretically, follow the trail of invoices backwards to the point of original manufacture if the goods are counterfeit or stolen; if, as may well be the case, the invoice trail is false one can, theoretically, accomplish the same end with street level surveillance. But the repeated seizure of street peddlers' wares makes no more of a dent in the illicit commerce in contraband goods than repeated arrests of street dealers stops the flow of narcotics into the United States, and that has not worked. However necessary it is for social purposes to combat street level distribution, it is more effective to deter crime at its source—with the wholesalers and manufacturers. To prove by evidence in a court of law who are the wholesalers and manufacturers there exist two choices.

One can attempt to follow the goods backwards from the point of sale to the point of origin, or one can follow the money from the point of sale back to the beneficiaries. There is a serious problem with tracing the origin of goods, aside from the investigative difficulty, and that has to do with the fact that certain goods, at some point in their origination, are legal until they are mislabeled, and hence are immune from effective seizure.[11] Proof of the receipt of profits, however, is evidence on which one can act. The money, by definition, is the proceeds of the sale of contraband, and hence is the proceeds of crime. By tracing the money to its ultimate beneficiaries

---

[10] And, of course, without the royalties or licensing fees there is little economic incentive for inventors, designers, composers, authors or even software writers to work. The condition of man in a state of nature, wrote Thomas Hobbes, is solitary, poor, nasty, brutish and short. The rule of law is an improvement ? for everyone.

[11] I have in mind, for example, watches which can be manufactured inexpensively, and legally, and do not acquire their counterfeit characteristics until a brand name is falsely attached. That step, which can be late in the process, leaves the expensive capital-intensive part of the manufacturing process immune from forfeiture. "How was I to know that the other scoundrel would add a false brand name?" will be the defense offered by a shipper even if he is corrupt and secretly pays the man who adds the false brand name to the watches.

one can both seize the money and make a legal case against the human beings who profit from the trade in counterfeit goods (or contraband weapons or drugs).

In that sense following the profits from contraband is far more lucrative and productive—financially and in terms of evidence obtained—than is the tracing of the goods themselves.

That solution, however, has a major failing, and it is one which needs to be addressed and remedied.

The problem with tracing money to identify the people engaged in profiting from contraband (and it would be the same if the money were being used to fund terrorism) is that there exist hurdles to obtaining valid, legal evidence. Key among the hurdles are bank secrecy laws, corporate secrecy laws and a wholesale use of what are euphemistically called "trusts.". To hold accountable in the world economy those people benefiting from economic crime, the secrecy that such laws foster must be abolished, at least as to law enforcement and anti-terrorism investigations.

## KEEPING UP WITH TECHNOLOGY

As the world economy becomes more like a global village we must adjust. We can not afford the peculiar legal quirks of places such as Grand Cayman, or the British Virgin Islands, which operate as havens of secrecy, whether for bank transactions or corporate ownership. The impact—indeed the purpose of those laws—is to facilitate money laundering for the purpose of concealing criminal activity. It is necessary to adjust our view of the equal sovereignty with which we have dignified many nations unworthy of equal treatment in world financial markets.[12] We need to provide for adequately staffed modern legal systems, adjusting to new technologies as technologies change. We need independent and honest prosecutors. We can not afford local corruption anywhere if it impacts on the world economy. As times change we must change with them.

Simply put, with our current technology it is possible to move money in and out of bank secrecy jurisdictions so fast that investigation becomes almost impossible. In the case of BCCI the bank secrecy statutes of the various jurisdictions in which BCCI operated were such that no one—no auditor, no regulator, indeed no one outside the circle of thieves—knew the true identities of the owners of the bank or of its various borrowers. Without that knowledge it is impossible to evaluate whether transactions are with related parties, or are arms-length deals in which a banker is putting his own money at risk, and is presumably using his best judgment in doing so. Old-fashioned secrecy is out of date. We must adapt.

I suggest that we do so by eliminating bank secrecy statutes as a factor in international trade and finance. In this age of multi-billion dollar a year narcotics trafficking, of 24 hour a day securities markets with international securities frauds as easy to accomplish as lifting the phone and calling abroad, and "asset protection programs" which are a euphonious way of describing frauds on creditors and courts, it is inappropriate for international lawyers and bank regulators to defend in the abstract that which is in reality used to corrupt the public and private lives of the major industrial and financial nations or the world.

## MONEY LAUNDERING AND NARCOTICS

Narcotics massively inflate the problems of violent crime, economic crime, and official corruption with which the District Attorney's office deals every day. The District Attorney's Office is on Centre Street, due south of Park Avenue in Manhattan. Park Avenue at the north of the island has a large population of narcotics addicts, who must burglarize, rob, and steal to feed their narcotics addiction. The money they get goes to drug dealers, to larger drug dealers, and then into the banking system. South from Harlem on Park Avenue are a large number of the world's banks; BCCI was there, at 320 Park, laundering narcotics money from the junkies committing crimes of theft and violence here. Due South of the District Attorney's Office is the Federal Reserve Bank of New York, where the dirty money was transferred. When we started investigating BCCI the District Attorney decided that bankers laundering narcotics money should be derailed by our office, and if possible sent to jail.

---

[12] For example, there was a proposal adopted that *all* financial transactions through Antigua, a notorious money-laundering nation be deemed suspicious, which requires any United States licensed financial institution to fill out Suspicious Activity Reports for every transaction involving that country. This tends to make their dealings very expensive, and highlights them all for law enforcement. Antigua responded by paying millions of dollars in a highly focused effort to enlist the support of key United States political leaders, who are in a political position to defeat the law enforcement efforts of the Department of State, the US Treasury, and the Department of Justice.

The money that went to BCCI had to get into the banking system, and then be invested, for the drug dealers to profit. Likewise the proceeds from the sale of counterfeit goods has got to get into the banking system for the counterfeiters to benefit. To keep their profits safe, and to keep law enforcement from getting legal evidence against them, the bad guys, be they thieves or counterfeiters, or narcotics dealers (who, after all, are merely homicidal businessmen dealing in unlicensed pharmaceutical products based on cocoa leaves and poppies) need secrecy, which means that they need to launder their money through a bank secrecy or a corporate secrecy jurisdiction—Grand Cayman, British Virgin Islands or the like—before sending it back to Park Avenue for investment. And what we have learned, as I mentioned earlier—and it is frightening—is that the money, once back in New York, is respectable, and can be used to buy influence over the law enforcement and foreign policy decisions of the United States and other nations.[13] The ancient concept used now to validate bank and corporate secrecy is that bank secrecy must be preserved to keep a gentleman's financial affairs confidential. That concept dates back to the days when only "gentlemen" had checking accounts. That concept is archaic, and must give way to the current reality. Bank secrecy statutes in international trade and finance are used by crooks, tax evaders, securities fraudsters, counterfeiters and capital flight fellows; they are used by narcotics dealers, but they are not needed by honest folks engaged in honest transactions.[14]

I have said that bank secrecy in international finance must give way to the harsh realities of life. There is no reason why the people on Grand Cayman can not have rigid bank secrecy laws. I for one do not care what they do amongst themselves, so long as they are consenting adults. I do care, however, when they try to merchant their sovereign status and impose their sovereignty on the rest of us to protect narco-dollars or other proceeds of contraband from detection. If the people of Grand Cayman, the British Virgin Islands, or the other countries selling their sovereignty for cash were to have bank secrecy statutes relating only to local residents—not corporations—doing business in their local currency, and not involved in international trade and finance, their laws would be of concern only to themselves. But we are not dealing with that.[15]

Banks in such countries are taking deposits from people they have never met and from brass-plate companies with no assets except the bank account, and inserting the money into the world monetary system. Most of this is in dollars, and most of it goes through Manhattan.

Two thirds of the world's trade is conducted in dollars. Far more than 95% of the international dollar transactions clear through New York County in any given day. The current volume, I understand, is about $2.7 trillion on a normal day. One can move that volume of money only by moving it so quickly that it is instantaneous. I remember my shock when I learned that the fastest way for two banks in Hong Kong to settle a dollar transaction was to wire the money from Hong Kong to New York and back again. What that means is that from an evidentiary point of view money in New York can be wired to Grand Cayman, sheltered from further identification, and wired back to New York as an arms-length transaction, when in fact it is not. That money's trip to Grand Cayman, economically harmless a century ago when it required a sailboat, gold coins, and handwritten entries, is infinitely mischievous when it can be done electronically, instantaneously, from a distance, with no one ever going to the island at all.[16]

---

[13] See footnote 4.

[14] There are three levels of bank "secrecy" which warrant discussion. There is an obvious interest in privacy - in that no one wants his financial affairs to be open to his competitors, his neighbors or perhaps, his family. At that level only bone-fide criminal investigators and bank regulators can get access to the data. At the next level of secrecy only bank regulators can get access to the identifying information on bank accounts and financial transactions; police officers can not. At the third level not even bank regulators can obtain the identifying information necessary to see if transactions involve relating parties or are being conducted at arms length.

[15] When Lichtenstein launders payments from the French government-owned oil company through North African nations and into the coffers of a political party in Germany, Lichtenstein becomes of concern to us all.

[16] One final note on the economic utility of tax havens. Countries, which exist to shelter in untaxed form profits earned from the world's industry and commerce, provide an exceptionally mischievous service which should not be tolerated. The following example comes to mind. A man owns a factory in London which produces widgets. He establishes a sales company offshore in the Caribbean and sells his widgets through that company. Before he established the sales company he made a profit let us say of a million pounds a year on which he paid taxes. After he established the sales company he sold goods at almost no profit from the factory to the sales company and sold the goods at whatever profits he could realize from the sales company to the world market. He paid no taxes. The factory in London still requires fire protection; the garbage must be collected; and he very much expects that the police will protect his premises from depre-

Technology has changed world trade and world finance irrevocably in recent years, and we must adjust to that change.

PRIVACY OF BANKING VS. ANONYMITY OF CRIME

Just as bank secrecy is a criminally malevolent anachronism, so too have secretly owned corporations and anonymous trusts become tools of the trade for the criminal parasites on the world economy. It is only slightly useful to be able to trace funds if the beneficiaries of those funds can conceal their identities. But, following the huge amounts of money involved in the narcotics trade, we have found an entire cottage industry of professionals—bankers, lawyers, accountants, and so-called financial planners—establishing ostensibly legal mechanisms for people to conceal the ownership of money from the courts of the nations in which they choose to live.

Let me give you an example. In one case a British part-time magistrate and his former partner, a lawyer, in London, established a whole series of companies to facilitate securities fraud in New York.

The way the scheme worked, a securities fraudster in New York hired the judge to set up off-shore companies to buy "Reg S stock," which companies could not be owned by someone who was an American citizen or resident, as the fraudster and his colleagues were. The judge and his partner incorporated the companies in Liberia, witout selecting an "owner" which worked for a while. But then the United States SEC came looking around to see who owned the companies. The British magistrate thereupon hired a Liberian diplomat to falsely state that he was the beneficial owner of the companies. As the diplomat had diplomatic immunity, one could reasonably assume that his statement would end the inquiry.[17]

These companies, having been established with no owner, could transfer ownership quite readily; one could transfer their entire assets (a bank account) by "selling" the company without anyone knowing that a transfer had occurred. That transaction, in slightly different form, takes place routinely in the laundering of money we believe originates in the drug trade, but the technique is clearly transferable. In fact, British police, following a narcotics money launderer, found much of the evidence about the Liberian companies. When we got together, by good fortune, the British police provided the evidence to convict our securities fraudsters: they in turn promptly gave evidence against the magistrate, whom the British police proceeded to arrest. It turned out that he had performed his "secret corporation" trick for a large number of people, including a number of New Yorkers.

In another case one of the big accounting firms established a corporation in the Caribbean, and acted as its managing agent. One of my colleagues at the District Attorney's office served the accounting firm with a subpoena, and the firm fatuously asserted that the Caribbean partnership was not the United States partnership, and that they had not been served. Of course both partnerships have the same name, the same signature, the same telephone book—internal—and the Caribbean partners who took direction from New York. So the firm agreed to accept service of the

---

dation by street criminals. His contribution to the cost of those services however is nil. To make matters worse the offshore company is audited if at all by accountants who care only about their audit and not about the expenses of the firm. The hiring of public servants working for countries off-shore to the tax havens for nominal work at high pay which ? might be construed by independent observers as bribes ? attracts no scrutiny and the tax laws continue to permit this sort of behavior.

The amount of wealth in offshore tax havens is enormous, it is liquid, it is immune from audit and most criminal investigations and it is available to malefactors of great wealth for malicious use without fear of retribution. Given the constant need of politicians the world over for money this pool constitutes a constant temptation to corrupt governments throughout the world while allocating the tax burden of the cost of governments to people without the ability to hide their wealth. The anti-democratic implications and the morally corrupting aspects of this behavior are just becoming known.

What is clear is that, here too, times change. The old idea that one country does not care about the fiscal offenses of another has outlived its usefulness; it is now dangerous. Some years ago, you will recall, the Russian government was so strapped for revenue that it had to go to the oligarchs asking them to pay their taxes. The billions of dollars laundered through the Bank of New York were tax evasion or tax avoidance, and "not really a problem for us." "Not a Problem" that is, until you realize that the Russian government has nuclear, chemical and biological weapons, that the people guarding those weapons need to be paid, and that there are terrorists in the world willing to buy the weapons. All of a sudden one understands that the collapse of the Russian government due to non-payment of taxes would be a disaster with worldwide consequences. Or simply, as one of our Supreme Court Justices wrote three quarters of a century ago, ?Taxes are what we pay for civilized society.?

[17] That it did not is due partly to luck and mostly to the skill of the detectives working on the case, who persuaded the diplomat to cooperate with law enforcement authorities.

subpoena, but then responded that they did not know who owned the company, and would have to ask the person with whom they dealt.

Such behavior by professionals is designed to make money out of crime. The lawyers and accountants are establishing formalistic structures specifically designed to defeat those very laws which we need to establish a level playing field. If thieves can hire accountants and attorneys to shield the proceeds of crime, there is a problem with the law.

Money laundering is the process of concealment. To trace the proceeds of crime you need legal, competent, valid evidence.[18] To the extent that contraband is, as it surely is, an attack on legitimate commerce, laws protecting the proceeds of contraband commerce are bad for the economy of the world. And, quite frankly, to the extent that professionals assist this conduct by establishing structures designed prospectively to defeat valid legal claims they too are our enemies.

Times change. The world economy is in flux, and will continue to be. The value of goods and services will vary over time. But if we are to establish a rule of law in the global economy we must forbid the bank secrecy and corporate secrecy laws and traditions which are so inimical to legal, honest, competent evidence—that is, inimical to the truth. Corporations which are creatures of law and are themselves law-abiding must work together to eliminate the use of bank secrecy, corporate secrecy, and other anachronistic legalisms used to shield the proceeds of crime from its victims.

Prior to the USA PATRIOT Act New York State implemented an anti-money laundering law, designed to prosecute the people in the business of laundering money. It was effective November 1, 2000, and applies only to the State of New York. As a state law it covers, among other institutions, the Federal Reserve Bank of New York, the Fedwire system, the Clearing House Association and the Clearing House Inter-Bank Payment System (CHIPS) as well as the clearing systems for almost all United States securities and government debt markets. If you deal in United States dollars, other than in currency form, the law affects your business.

The law forbids the laundering through New York of the proceeds of crime, whether the crime took place in New York or in any other jurisdiction. Put simply the law forbids the laundering of the proceeds of specified criminal conduct, whether involving drugs, tax crimes, or other criminal conduct. If the laundering is of drug money, the level of the offense varies with the amount of money. If the criminal conduct involves tax fraud or securities fraud or other criminal conduct, the amounts of money are higher than if drugs were involved, to achieve the same degree of crime.

Besides forbidding the laundering of the proceeds of a broad variety of crimes through New York, the statute specifically forbids the use of the payments and settlements systems to avoid reporting requirements or to advance new crimes. And the law provides that if a financial institution is told that certain funds are the proceeds of what is called "Specified criminal conduct" and the institution engages in the financial transactions anyway, the financial institution is at risk.

And in determining the regulatory climate towards money laundering in New York it is easiest to say that the new law was passed with the strong support of the New York State Banking Department and the Federal Reserve Bank of New York, the two key regulators in the State.

It was proposed by the New York County District Attorney, Robert M. Morgenthau, who personally lobbied the Legislature to get the bill passed. It is, even now, being enforced.

But laws are not sufficient. We need to persuade other countries to work together with us. The process of persuasion is far different from our dictating what must happen. And in the rational discourse that should attend efforts at persuasion I believe that, for the most part, there are exceedingly strong arguments for an end to the legal tangles caused by bank secrecy, corporate secrecy, and the unbridled use of trusts to conceal the identities of persons moving funds internationally.

As I stated earlier money is power. The ability to move money secretly is the ability to exercise power without responsibility. In this day and age we all live too closely together to permit secrecy concerns for taxes or the like to shelter the identity of the wealthiest felons in the world.

It is worth mentioning that the world financial system is complex. Very few prosecutors understand it; few people examine the flows of funds to see what is happening in the world. The technicians who understand how money is moved, not the compliance departments in the largest institutions, are the people who, if they are

[18] I say legal because you can, by paying money or otherwise, unlawfully obtain the information from a "bank secrecy" jurisdiction. You just can not use it in court. The rule of law providing for secrecy becomes a rule protecting only the guilty.

persuaded to combat money laundering, can do so. But little effort has been made, as far as I know, to educate the technicians on the evils attendant on their money funds without leaving a trace.

A few months ago I was speaking with a European banker from a smaller institution, who was in the business of paying and receiving United States dollars to and from Cuba, in the face of economic sanctions. The mechanics were interesting. He would send dollars to, say, a Venezuelan bank by making a bank to bank transfer through New York. Cuban names, bank accounts, and other identifying information would simply not appear on the transfer. He would also send a SWIFT message to the Venezuelan Bank, not through the United States, instructing his Venezuelan banker to put the money into the account of the Cuban bank or company.

So much for that bank and sanctions against Cuba.

If we persuade the banking industry to stop using the bulk bank-to-bank transfers—the SWIFT 202s—we will establish better control over the ultimate beneficiary of the money being moved. But we can not implement such a rule without achieving consensus that it is a good idea. Just as laws depend on the consent of the governed, sanctions can work if they are kept simple, and the cause is perceived to be just. Sanctions can not be implemented and forgotten; the arguments in favor of any sanctions must be kept fresh, and made as often as necessary to keep people persuaded that sanctions, a step short of war, should be maintained.

Thank you.

Mr. ROHRABACHER. Thank you very much, and will return for some questions momentarily.

## STATEMENT OF JONATHAN M. WINER, ESQ., PARTNER, ALSTON & BIRD, LLP

Mr. WINER. Thank you, Mr. Chairman. This is an Oversight and Investigations Subcommittee. I am going to speak to those issues, and I also want to address the sanctions issue raised earlier.

Sanction busting is a very big issue for this country. When economic sanctions are widely adopted, they have an impact. When they are adopted by the U.S. alone, they can usually be circumvented and circumvented easily. It is easy for targets of sanctions to bust them when the foreign country does not honor them. Iran is a perfect example. Bank Melli Iran, a state-owned institution; go on the Web. You can find out their correspondent banks. They have correspondent bank relationships in Bahrain, France, Germany, Hong Kong, Oman, the UAE (United Arab Emirtes), and the United Kingdom. The entity that has those relationships is a UK subsidiary of the Iranian bank.

Another one that I want to bring your attention to: Bank Sepah is lovely because if you go on their Web site, not only do they have correspondent banks in the UAE, Australia, Canada, Switzerland, Denmark, Germany, the UK, Hong Kong, Japan, Norway, and Sweden; they say, oh, if you want to be in dollars, by the way, call and inquire. If you need to get it through the United States, call and inquire. Now that is available online.

Similarly, the United States has long imposed sanctions on Cuba. If a United States person wants to wire funds to Cuba, all he or she has to do is to go to a bank in Canada, including some that advertise on the Web, and wire funds to that bank, use a hush mail account or another closed e-mail account, tell them to keep your records over there, and use that foreign bank account, which you report on your 1040, Schedule B—you have not violated that law—to do whatever you want, including send funds to Cuba. It is going to be almost impossible for the United States to find out. That is merely one mechanism. There are lots of others. The fundamental problem: Canada does not believe in the sanctions, nor does the

EU. It makes them essentially impossible to enforce. My testimony goes into more detail as to how you go about violating those sanctions if you want to.

So given all of this, where might the Subcommittee consider spending its time? By the way, I would endorse pretty much everything that has been said by my counterparts on this table. First, the Subcommittee can, and should, investigate key nodes of illicit finance. The Treasury has indicated some of these nodes publicly: Latvia, northern Cyprus, and Burma. I believe the issue of how Iran moves its funds through international banks remains an important area for further exploration and one where Congress could play a significant role.

I would also still love to know where Saddam Hussein got his Iraqi currency. The amazing thing about the investigation that you looked at this morning is that it identified Iranian currency, Cuban currency, and what was the other one, Burmese currency perhaps? It never answered the question of where all of those fresh dollar bills came in Iraq. I think we ought to know. I do not know the answer, but we ought to. Somebody ought to be investigating it.

Secondly, investigate cases of international corruption. This Subcommittee could play an important role by focusing on illicit financing in jurisdictions where corruption and other financial crime relating to money laundering could have a particularly significant impact on the United States. One possible focus of such an investigation could be the banking system of China, which has long struggled with the problem of money laundering and corruption embedded in many of its major financial institutions. Other possible candidates for such investigative efforts, in addition to Iran, would be Pakistan and Nigeria.

It is worth, as my colleagues have suggested, focusing efforts on compliance in weak jurisdictions, in some of the smaller jurisdictions. Section 311 of the USA PATRIOT Act is a very powerful tool. The Treasury has barely used it, has been afraid to use it. The market access consequences of its use are immediate and profound. People respond to Section 311 designations almost instantaneously.

Mr. ROHRABACHER. Could you repeat what you just said, that last sentence?

Mr. WINER. Section 311 designations create limitations on market access to foreign financial institutions or, more broadly, the economic systems of a country that have been designated if a country is designated. It is not IEEPA (International Emergency Economic Powers Act) sanctions. It is not national security sanctions. It is PATRIOT Act sanctions, a powerful tool that Congress gave the Administration after September 11. It has been used a little. It will probably be used more.

Similarly, the PATRIOT Act gives the power, further, and the Administration has the power under IEEPA, the International Emergency Economic Powers Act, to designate a foreign financial institution or a business that facilitates terrorist finance as a supporter of global terrorism and freeze those assets. You can even freeze those assets using long-arm jurisdiction that the Congress gave the Administration. So if you have the assets at a foreign bank that touches the United States, you go to the foreign bank, and you say, “Sorry, Foreign Bank. We know you have got the assets of that guy over there in that country. We are grabbing that amount of assets here in the United States. You can make it up over there." We barely use that.

The President has issued an Executive Order saying he is going to go after companies that facilitate WMD (Weapons of Mass Destruction) proliferation and put them as designees under IEEPA. That is a very significant action taken by the President. I would like to see the intelligent community and law enforcement agencies and regulators working with the Administration to use that very aggressively, and, again, Iran might be a terrific opportunity for further use in that regard, and this Subcommittee could do investigative work in that area that might facilitate it.

Finally, developing systems for regulating gold, diamonds, and other barter commodities used by terrorists needs to be done. There has been insufficient work doing it. This Subcommittee could focus on it. Reviewing the regulation of free zones, developing global standards for free zones—another area that people have just failed to undertake to this point. Reviewing the international regulation of charities is still an area that requires further work that has not been done.

Finally, I note that Congress, in 2001, passed the PATRIOT Act calling on the Administration to enact regulations comprehensively affecting all financial institutions within 12 months. It is now four and a half years later. There are significant sectors that are still not the subject of regulations. That invites regulatory arbitrage.

"Regulatory arbitrage" means that if a bank cannot do it, but a hedge fund can because a bank is regulated, and a hedge fund is not, I am going to do it in the hedge fund. That is regulatory arbitrage. That is merely one example. There are no hedge fund regulations now on money laundering. If you are a hedge fund, you have no antimoney laundering obligations right now. Proposed regs only. It has been four and a half years.

Finally, the criticality of traceability, which my colleagues referred to. There is no reason for any country in the world to be permitted to use the common plumbing, the common financial infrastructure that we all use to move money around the world, without guaranteeing that funds can be traced from beginning to end when something goes wrong, whether it goes wrong from sanctions busting, a terrorist, a drug money launderer, a spouse hiding money from a husband, or a wife hiding money from their ex-spouse. It does not matter. The transactions need to be traceable, and the information needs to be shared, and the U.S. foreign policy should be focused on that goal because there are a lot of goals that can be accomplished not just for the United States but for a lot of other countries that cannot tolerate what we can tolerate because they are not as wealthy, if we were to focus on that. Thank you very much for your attention.

[The prepared statement of Mr. Winer follows:]

PREPARED STATEMENT OF JONATHAN M. WINER, ESQ., PARTNER, ALSTON & BIRD, LLP

Mr. Chairman and Members of the Subcommittee:

I am pleased to be here to discuss the role of offshore banks and their relationship to capital flight, money laundering, and other illegal activities, including their support of terrorism. I am also happy to provide you my understanding of how international banks have assisted U.S.-sanctioned countries in circumventing U.S. sanctions regimes. My understanding is based on some 20 years of experience working in this field, including undertaking investigations in this area during my service for the other Congressional body, and my six years as Deputy Assistant U.S. Secretary of State for International Law Enforcement from 1994–1999, prior to my becoming a partner at Alston & Bird, LLP, where my legal practice includes a significant focus on money laundering, sanctions, terrorist finance, corrupt payments, and related issues. In my testimony, I will address in brief each of the issues you have asked me to cover sequentially.

THE HISTORIC ROLE OF OFFSHORE BANKS

During the 1990s, U.S. policymakers and some of their European counterparts had come to recognize that offshore banks had essentially no meaningful controls in place to prevent money laundering. Such banks were typically "ring-fenced," meaning that they offered services only to non-resident of the countries in which they were incorporated. Thus, in return for a fee, a foreign person could place funds into an account in a bank secrecy haven that would refuse to cooperate with law enforcement and regulators from their home country. The account was typically opened in the name of a trust or other shell entity, in turn was managed by nominees. In some cases, the shares of the shell entity would be bearer shares, so that no one could prove the beneficial ownership of the accounts. We used to refer to this practice as "renting sovereignty," and many of those trying to combat it viewed it as a form of state-sponsored piracy.

Such a system was designed for tax evasion and capital flight, and used aggressively and effectively from the dawn of the era of international electronic banking and payments systems in the early 1980's to the close of the 20th Century by Colombian drug traffickers, Russian oligarchs, Nigerian and Filipino kleptocrats, Serbian genocidaires, and sanctions-busters alike. In that period, international banks, functioning mostly as "off-shore" jurisdictions by providing services to non-residents, provided continuing technical services to a wide range of practical destabilizers. Periodic eruptions of scandal revealed that drug and arms money launderers, diamond and timber smugglers, traffickers in people, terrorists, and corrupt officials chose a similar range of institutions to move and maintain their funds. These institutions typically included (a) small international business companies or trusts, established in jurisdictions of convenience, which establish (b) bank accounts at local financial institutions, which have correspondent banking relationships with (c) major international financial institutions, which (d) move funds willy-nilly throughout the world without regard to the provenance of the funds. The infrastructure for non-transparent international finance has nodes that have specialized in particular kinds of services. For example, until recently, the Bahamas and the Virgin Islands were among the world's principal creators of anonymous international business companies ("IBCs"). The Channel Islands, Gibraltar, and the Dutch Antilles were world-class centers for the establishment of trusts to hide the true ownership of funds. A single firm in Liechtenstein laundered political slush funds for ruling political parties in France and Germany; arms purchases for civil wars in Liberia and Sierra Leone; drug money for Ecuadorian cocaine trafficker Jose Reyes-Torres, and stolen funds for various West African dictators. The Liechtenstein example is not unique. Financial nodes that initially provide services for one purpose, such as tax evasion, over time attract more sinister illicit purposes.

As an increasing number of significant global problems became linked to illicit finance, money laundering had become recognized during the 1990's as a global problem requiring a global response. Prior to September 11, this response included new international instruments, such as the 2000 United Nations Convention to Combat Transnational Organized Crime; the Second Money Laundering Directive, issued by the European Union in late 2001; and the Financial Action Task Force ("FATF") and Organization for Economic Cooperation and Development ("OECD") name and shame exercises. Notably, the major self-regulatory organizations, such as the Basel Committee for Banking Supervision ("BGBS"), the International Organization of Securities Commissions ("IOSCO"), and the International Association of Insurance Supervisors ("IAIS") had also focused on extending standards for international regulation to cover transparency issues. The new standards were designed to respond to the major failures of existing financial regulation to provide protection against illegal activities. Each organization focused on major gaps in the international regulatory system that had translated into injuries to domestic supervision and enforcement. These gaps included:

- Fragmented supervision, within countries by sector, and among countries by national jurisdiction.

- Exploitation of differences among national laws to use regulatory arbitrage to circumvent more stringent national laws and international standards.
- Secrecy laws which impede the sharing of information among countries and between regulators and law enforcement.
- Inadequate attention to electronic payments in existing anti-money laundering supervision and enforcement, including "know your customer" rules, that focus on currency, even as the world's financial services businesses rapidly continue their move into E-money.
- The lack of international standards governing key mechanisms used in transnational financial transactions, such as international business companies ("IBCs"), off-shore trusts, off-shore insurance and reinsurance companies, and off-shore fund vehicles, including but not limited to hedge funds.
- Minimal due diligence by company formation agents, attorneys, and financial institutions in the process of incorporating and licensing of new financial institutions and shell companies and trusts owned by their affiliates.

In response, there was a convergence as to what the standards must be to protect many countries against many simultaneous threats. In essence, the standards had begun to require a form of "know your customer" at both the front end and the back end of any transaction. At the front end, bankers and other financial facilitators had become required to know with whom they are dealing, and at some level, what there customers have been doing with their money. At the back end, those permitting withdrawals of funds have needed to know not only who has been getting the money, but where it came from. That way, should something go wrong, the funds can be traced.

Requiring financial institutions to "know your customer," and countries to share bank records with one another in cases involving financial crime, are at the core of the international money laundering and terrorist finance enforcement and regulatory regime that has begun to be built over the past decade. This principle became embedded in the work of the G–7 Financial Stability Forum, of the EU's Third Directive on Money Laundering, effective last year, and in the USA–PATRIOT Act, enacted after September 11. These new legal regimes no longer treat all bank accounts as inherently equal, but require those who handle the funds of others to know who the beneficial owner is of an account, regardless of the nature of the account. In cases where an account is established through a jurisdiction that is inadequately regulated, or designed to hide beneficial ownership, these regimes would shut off access entirely.

In the period from 1999 through 2004, the U.S. participated in naming and shaming a number of jurisdictions, in providing evaluation, training and technical assistance to many more jurisdictions, and thereby contributing substantially to a very great change in the prevailing banking practices. In brief, "ring fencing," or the provision of services by banks solely to non-residents, became generally deemed to be unacceptable, and has been dramatically attenuated. Exchange of bank records instead of being a rarity, became increasingly commonplace. And the U.S. risk from shell banks and under-regulated jurisdictions became substantially more manageable.

## BANKS AND CAPITAL FLIGHT

Capital flight is the phenomenon of money leaving a country as a matter of avoiding political risk or taxation, or of receiving higher rates of returns elsewhere. It is ordinarily a sign that the economic and governance conditions in the country from which the capital is fleeing are uncertain or deteriorating. In recent years, we have seen massive amounts of capital flight from the countries of the former Soviet Union, from much of sub-Saharan Africa, and from elites in Latin America and Asia at times of political upheaval. It is normal for banks to want to serve wealthy customers, and jurisdictions such as Cyprus, the Channel Islands, the Bahamas, Singapore, Gibraltar, and Liechtenstein became prominent providers of financial services for such capital flight.

Provision of services for capital flight has been a somewhat subtler process than the provision of ring-fenced offshore services to criminals, and less susceptible to regulation. To this day, the process of capital flight continues to be facilitated by banks. Very often this takes place through legitimate banks accepting what appear to be legitimate proceeds of transactions involving international trade, especially natural resources. The technique of under-invoicing for goods allows an exporter to generate funds outside of a country and thus free from taxation and regulation. The technique of over-invoicing for goods allows an expert to send additional funds out of the country to a confederate or to a shell company under the guise of an arms-length transaction, and thereby similarly to create funds off-shore. Preventing these kinds of frauds is very difficult, and requires a great of cooperation among competent—and honest—customs officials in the countries involved. Needless to say, competent, honest customs officials are not always present in countries experiencing substantial levels of capital flight.

MONEY LAUNDERING AND CORRUPTION

The world's kleptocrats, whether Marcos, Mubuto, Abacha, or Sukarto, have used a common financial services infrastructure to steal national wealth. Grand corruption has been a prominent feature of political and social conflict or civic breakdown in Albania, Argentina, Burma, Cambodia, Congo (Zaire), Colombia, Haiti, Indonesia, Iran, Liberia, Nigeria, Panama, Pakistan, Peru, the Philippines, Romania, Sierra Leone, Yugoslavia, and Zimbabwe, among other jurisdictions. In each case, the looting of government treasuries has involved funds or resources residing within these countries being moved from the countries to other jurisdictions through the world's major international banks. In some cases, the theft of national treasuries has been accompanied by other harmful activities, whose proceeds have been laundered by the same mechanisms. These include costly or illegal arms deals (Angola, Colombia, Liberia, Sierra Leone, Somalia, Sudan), the smuggling of diamonds used to purchase arms deals in civil wars (Angola, Liberia, and Sierra Leone), grand-scale theft of oil and timber (Burma, Cambodia, Nigeria, Russia, Thailand), illegal dumping of environmental toxics (Guyana, Suriname), and embezzlement or other abuses of funds lent by international financial institutions such as the World Bank (endemic).

Countries that during the 1990's saw their national wealth disappear to other jurisdictions at the direction of ruling kleptocrats include (from A to Z):

- Albania, decapitalized by a pyramid scheme that moved its funds to Italy and Western Europe;
- Angola, whose immense national resources vanished amid the ongoing civil war between President Dos Santos and Jonas Savimbi;
- Burma, where funds generated by narcotics, jewels, and illicit timber were exported for covert reinvestment in more business friendly environments such as Singapore and Hong Kong by people working with the junta;
- Cambodia, which featured similar features of first generating illicit funds and then having them become flight capital under Hung Sen;
- Estonia, which found substantial amounts of its national wealth apparently transferred to Russia in the mid-1990's in a pyramid scheme arranged by a prominent banker with close ties to Latvia's then government;
- Gabon, whose oil revenues were sent offshore and handled by U.S financial institutions on behalf of senior leaders who had stolen the proceeds;
- Indonesia, where billions of dollars disappeared offshore in connection with grand corruption under former dictator Suharto, with some $9 billion ending up in a nominee account maintained at an Austrian bank;
- Kazakstan, where funds from oil revenues were laundered offshore for the benefit of senior leaders;
- Mexico, where the brother of president Carlos Salinas, Raul Salinas, was found to have moved at least hundreds of millions of dollars representing either stolen government funds, bribes, or the proceeds of narcotics trafficking, to Switzerland;
- Nigeria, where General Sani Abacha stole billions that were then stored in major banks in Luxembourg, the U.K., Liechtenstein, Switzerland and the Channel Islands, among other locations;
- Pakistan, where military rule replaced democratic civilian rule after hundreds of millions of the proceeds of corruption were found in Swiss banks, discrediting the elected Prime Minister and her family;
- Russia, whose financial system collapsed in 1999 amid massive money laundering overseas through the Caribbean, the South Pacific, New York, and London;
- Serbia, whose wealth was converted to the control of Slobodan Milosevic and his wife through such jurisdictions as Cyprus and Lebanon, while Serbia was subject to global sanctions by the United Nations;
- Ukraine, where substantial stolen assets of the state were found to have been laundered to the United States under the control of a former prime minister, after being handled by a number of Swiss banks;

- Zaire (Congo), whose national wealth was exported by the late dictator Mobuto to Swiss banks.

TERRORIST FINANCE

International terrorism represents an obvious threat to global security, just as domestic terrorism does to individual nations. In every case, terrorist organizations need to generate, store, and transport funds, often across borders. While not every domestic terrorist organization needs to launder money through cross-border transfers, over time, many such organizations choose to locate portions of their infrastructure at some distance away from planned terrorist activities. To do so, they establish cells to operate in jurisdictions separate from those where their political base is, or where their operations will be carried out. Prior to September 11, multinational movements of terrorist funds, involving the use of major international financial institutions have been traced to terrorist movements based in Afghanistan, Burma, Chechnya, Colombia, Israel, the Palestinian Territory, Kosovo, Lebanon, Northern Ireland, Pakistan, Papua-New Guinea, the Philippines, Somalia, Sri Lanka, Sudan, and Turkey. Although the terrorist organizations based in each of these countries have some level of minority popular support, their power and effectiveness have been leveraged by their ability to hide, invest, and transport their funds through the world's international financial institutions. A summary of the nations whose banks were used to handle funds for Al-Qaeda's attacks prior to September 11 instructive. Available public sources show Al Qaeda and related groups to have been able to move funds to institutions in the following countries: Albania, Australia, Austria, the Bahamas, Belgium, Canada, the Caymans, Cyprus, France, Germany, Greece, Hong Kong, Indonesia, Iraq, Italy, Kosovo, Kuwait, Libya, Macao, Malaysia, Malta, Mauritius, the Netherlands, Nigeria, Panama, Pakistan, the Philippines, Poland, Qatar, Saudi Arabia, the Seychelles, Singapore, Somalia, South Africa, Sudan, Switzerland, the United Arab Emirates, the United Kingdom, the United States, and Yemen.

But all of that was pre-September 11. Do international banks knowingly move terrorist funds today? The short, simple answer is "no." The down-sides are huge, and the banks make very serious efforts to avoid handling such funds, backed up by a harmonized international regime of know-your-customer and the customer's activities, UN and U.S. lists of sanctioned persons and entities, customer identification requirements, and suspicious transaction reporting requirements. But does that mean that the terrorists cannot move their funds? Certainly they can.

Today, the movements of terrorist funds involve a significant amount of cash couriers moving bulk currency from sources to recipients. Such funds also move to some extent through alternative remittance mechanisms such as halawadars, otherwise known as informal value transfer systems, usually operating in ethnic communities. It is not yet clear whether terrorists are taking advantage of new online payment mechanisms using the Internet to move funds through one-time-use facilities that do not require customer identification, but such mechanisms would likely be usable by terrorist groups sending funds to a cell in a different country. For similar reasons, stored value cards, in which one can load money at a merchant location for use at an ATM machine anywhere in the world, have an obvious terrorist finance potential. Again, it is not yet possible to determine whether this mechanism is actually being used for this purpose.

SANCTIONS BUSTING

The U.S. has long had vigorous programs of economic sanctions that apply to U.S. based financial institutions under the Trading With the Enemy Act ("TWEA"), applied for more than 40 years to Cuba, and under the International Emergency Economic Powers Act ("IEEPA"), applied to many different countries, organizations, and individuals over the past 25 years. Economic sanctions are intended to deprive the target of the use of its assets and deny the target access to the U.S. financial system and the benefits of trade, transactions and services involving U.S. markets. These financial sanctions have had widely varying effectiveness, with the degree of effectiveness heavily related to their degree of universality. Those adopted widely often have an impact. When they have been adopted by the U.S. alone, they have generally been widely circumvented.

In a nutshell, it is easy for targets of sanctions to bust sanctions if a foreign country does not honor them. For example, the government of Iran has long been subject to financial sanctions in the U.S. Yet Bank Melli Iran, one of the Iranian government's major state owned institutions, has an extensive international network of correspondent banking relationships, with branches and offices in Azerbaijan, Bahrain, France, Germany, Hong Kong, Russia, Oman, the UAE and the United Kingdom. In practice, there is very little, if anything, that Iran cannot obtain in the international markets with this kind of access to international banks—access that is provided as a matter of state policy by the governments concerned. The Iranian bank, Bank Sepah, has a UK subsidiary that advertises itself as "truly international in character with relationships in over 45 countries worldwide," whose main business trade finance for Iranian exports and imports, with correspondent banks in the UAE, Australia, Canada, Switzerland, Denmark, Germany, the UK, Hong Kong, Japan, Norway, Sweden—and the U.S.—though for that relationship one is required to "call and inquire."

Similarly, the U.S. has long imposed sanctions on Cuba. Yet if a U.S. person wants to wire funds to Cuba, all he or she has to do is to a bank in Canada, including some that advertise on the web, and wire funds to that bank. For example, funds are transferred to Cuba via Canada-based Transcard from secure bank accounts in Canada. Similar businesses located in Europe, such as Spain and Italy-based SerCuba and Switzerland-based AWS Technologies, are proliferating. The problem is that other countries do not support the U.S. on these sanctions, making them effectively unenforceable.

If I choose to engage in sanctions busting, it would be very easy for me to do so without getting caught. I could open up a bank account in a foreign country, such as Canada, that does not abide by the particular sanction. I would duly report that account on my federal income tax forms, thereby abiding by U.S. tax reporting laws. I would wire funds to that account. And then, using an anonymous and encrypted e-mail account, and there are many such services my personal computer, I would instruct the foreign bank to wire funds to the sanctioned country, and to send me records pertaining to that account solely to my secret, anonymous, encrypted e-mail account.

The key for the U.S. to avoid this scenario is simple: obtain international support for the sanction involved. Because unilateral sanctions simply are no longer sustainable in a global environment.

## OPPORTUNITIES FOR INVESTIGATION AND OVERSIGHT

In light of the complexity of the uses of offshore banks and international banks for illicit finance of one kind or another, and the advanced state of the multiple ongoing initiatives to discourage such use, what opportunities may exist for this Committee to undertake investigative and oversight work in this field? I suggest this committee consider the following options:

### *1. Investigate Key Nodes of Illicit Finance.*

I respectfully suggest that there remain important nodes for illicit activity that may be worth focused attention by this Committee, with its international jurisdiction. The Treasury has indicated some of these nodes publicly, those in Latvia, Northern Cyprus, and Burma. I believe that the issue of how Iran moves its funds through international banks remains an important area for further exportation, and one where Congress could play a significant role. Treasury officials may be willing to identify other such nodes to this Committee behind closed doors. Investigations by the Committee into the correspondent banking relationships, historic and current, relating to these jurisdictions, of international banks, could well illuminate how bad actors are able to move funds internationally in the face of sanctions designed to prevent them from so doing. Similarly, if the Committee wishes to understand sanctions busting better, it can bring in the Federal Reserve and Treasury officials who have looked most closely at how the sanctions busting was done, and through investigation and oversight, assess additional steps that could be taken to respond.

### *2. Investigate Cases of International Corruption.*

The other Congressional body carried out important oversight work in the years 2000–2002 on the issue of money laundering and corruption by focusing on particular jurisdictions. At this time, this Committee could play an important role by focusing on illicit finance relating to jurisdictions where corruption and other financial crime relating to money laundering could have a particularly significant impact on the United States. One possible focus of such an investigation could be the banking system of China, which has long struggled with the problem of money laundering and corruption. Other possible candidates for such investigative efforts could include Iran, Pakistan, and Nigeria.

### *3. Focus Efforts on Compliance In Weak Jurisdictions*

Having reviewed key nodes, this Committee could look at which jurisdictions continue to have inadequate compliance measures in place, and could recommend the

U.S. government consider further actions to isolate the financial institutions of any countries that fail to address money laundering and terrorist finance sufficiently. Treasury has this power under Section 311 of the Patriot Act. To date it has been used sparingly and not at all in relationship to financial institutions in the Middle East. It may well be that further Congressional attention to Section 311 authorities and their use could result in additional focus by the Administration and by foreign governments on the implications of this tool.

*4. Proceed With Designations of Foreign Financial Institutions and Businesses as Facilitators of Terrorist Finance or Nuclear Proliferation.*

If we have any information regarding a foreign bank or business providing assistance or support to a terrorist group, our government should use its sanctions authority to designate such an institution. This has been done rarely since 2001, and again, tailored use of this tool could well leverage U.S. power. There is an especially significant opportunity to sue this tool in connection with the President's Executive Order regarding sanctions against persons and entities facilitating WMD proliferation. The Congress could play a useful focus in focusing the world's attention on this Executive Order and the entities against whom it could be used.

*5. Develop Systems for Regulating Gold, Diamonds, and Other Barter Commodities Used By Terrorists.*

It is in the interests of our government to understand how terrorists use commodities in conjunction with hawalas and other alternative remittance systems to go around the formal system of banking and thereby to fund terrorism. Our understanding of these areas remains inadequate. The need for understanding them and then developing systems for marking and regulation is critical for us to make it harder for terrorists to evade oversight. The pioneering work done by the Drug Enforcement Administration ("DEA") in understanding the black market peso exchange, which involved money laundering through commodities as well as alternative remittance systems may be a useful place to begin in this analysis. Ultimately, we will need regulatory regimes covering these additional sectors, applied on a global basis through the FATF.

*6. Review the Regulation of Free Zones and Develop Global Standards.*

The world's free zones have long been vulnerable to money laundering, due to their relative lack of customs controls. The Gulf States today have some prominent free trade zones, multiple mechanisms for alternative and informal payment systems, and these are adjacent to gold markets. Panama's Colon Free Zone has demonstrated that this combination is susceptible to money laundering abuse. Yet to date there is no global set of regulations applying to free zones to deal with money laundering and terrorist finance vulnerabilities. While regulation and review of free trade zones may today in the first instance be in the jurisdiction of other Committees, attention should be given to thinking through the intersection of the payments systems and trade documentation at the free trade zones to determine whether the zones today pose special vulnerabilities for terrorist finance.

*7. Review International Regulation of Charities.*

Review the international regulation of charities. Terrorist groups continue to seize on charities as a means of raising and moving funds and logistical support. As NSC terrorist finance chief Juan Zarate has testified before Congress, "the infrastructure of charitable organizations and their geographic scope have enabled terrorist groups to shift funds, supporters and operatives around the world quietly through charities." The U.S. has worked to develop case studies and typologies of terrorist abuse of charities, working closely with the Financial Action Task Force ("FATF"). It has also developed measures that donors and charities can use to protect themselves, releasing the "Anti-Terrorist Financing Guidelines: Voluntary Best Practices for U.S. Based Charities," which it released in November 2002. Mr. Chairman, these voluntary measures are fine. But they are voluntary. They should be mandatory. Charities should be no less responsible for combating terrorist finance than are financial institutions. We require banks, mutual funds, money services businesses, broker/dealers, investment advisers, and many other categories of financial institutions to put anti-money laundering policies and procedures in place as a condition of license. We are in the processing of requiring insurance companies, which are state-regulated, loan or finance companies, which are largely unregulated, and hedge funds, which by definition are not subject to regulation, to put these policies and procedures into place. And yet we have done nothing to require charities—which are tax exempt institutions and required to file documentation with the IRS to maintain that status—to put anti-money laundering policies and procedures in place.

If the voluntary standards are worth anything, they should be more than voluntary. The problem with charities funding terrorism has not been limited to foreign charities, but has involved charities based in the U.S. In an affidavit filed in U.S. federal court, U.S. Customs Agent David Kane cites a recent CIA report made public in response to a FOIA request, which states that of more than 50 Islamic nongovernmental organizations in existence in 1996, "available information indicates that approximately one-third of these Islamic NGOs support terrorist groups or employ individuals who are suspected of having terrorist connections." We should put into place regulations of charities similar to that of other businesses we have found to have substantial risk of money laundering or terrorist finance, with at least a baseline of anti-money laundering and terrorist finance policies and procedures made a condition of tax exempt status. We should then move to have that approach implemented internationally.

I thank you for providing me the opportunity to testify and remain available to respond to your questions.

Mr. DELAHUNT. Mr. Chairman, if I could, that was great testimony.

Mr. ROHRABACHER. Your may proceed.

Mr. DELAHUNT. I am going to excuse myself for 10 or 15 minutes. I shall return. I just have a few questions.

Mr. ROHRABACHER. It is unfortunate. This was just the 10 minutes I was going to ask about Halliburton.

Mr. DELAHUNT. I will check that record.

Mr. ROHRABACHER. Well, thank you all for your terrific testimony. A couple of things here. Mr. Evans, you talked about small money, money in small amounts being clean money, then going bad, as being perhaps the biggest component of the problem that we are looking at. What about big money that is basically drug money? Here we have, whether it is in Latin America or elsewhere, billions of dollars of drug money. Is not this a major component?

Mr. EVANS. Absolutely. It is a major component, and it is a major problem, but it is a different problem. The problem we have with criminal proceeds, whether it is from drugs or from stolen money, of tracing that money and recovering it is a very different kind of a problem than having mechanisms in place where we can prevent money coming into the country for bad purposes. The amount of money used to finance September 11th—I have heard the number, but it is very modest, a couple of hundred thousand dollars or something like that. It is a different problem. I am not suggesting one is a problem and the other is not, just that it is a different problem.

Mr. ROHRABACHER. Knowing those types of operations, I will tell you that it might have cost a couple of hundred thousand dollars for just the specifics of it, but in the setting up and the running of al-Qaeda during that time, the operations that were needed to support that, we are talking about tens of millions.

Mr. EVANS. Offshore, yes.

Mr. ROHRABACHER. Yes. The actual buying of tickets or something like that for somebody, paying for their hotel room or whatever was minimal, but that was a very well-financed operation. By the way, does anyone here know exactly where that money came from? Where did that money come from that paid for the training of the pilots, the keeping of the pilots, the communication, the sustaining of these 19 terrorist individuals who ended up slaughtering 3,000 Americans? Where did that money originally come from? What bank was being used to transfer it? Do we know that? Mr. Winer?

Mr. WINER. Well, there are two phases that have been publicly identified. One is it moved through a financial institution in Dubai. It then went to a United States financial institution based in south Florida, where the terrorist involved got multiple ATM cards from that U.S. financial institution.

Mr. ROHRABACHER. And what was that financial institution? Do you remember, in Florida?

Mr. WINER. Yes. It was Sun Trust. That is 5 years ago, and that bank, like other banks, has put into place the requirements of the PATRIOT Act since, so it is not something, at this point, you should blame anybody for; it is what happened.

Mr. ROHRABACHER. Right. It was a respected financial institution that people played within the rules and were able to set up a financial system for a major terrorist operation in the United States.

Mr. WINER. The funds clearly moved through a number of financial institutions along the way of which those two happened to be identified.

Mr. ROHRABACHER. So, first and foremost, if we are talking about this in light of 9/11, is to make sure that we have a system where American banks and people who are on the up and up, that we set a standard so that they cannot be manipulated by other international institutions. Go right ahead, Mr. Moscow.

Mr. MOSCOW. The problem here is that we have international debit cards so that you can open an account abroad and use a debit card to pay your living expenses, draw cash against it and so on, and there is no need for the bank account to be in the United States anymore.

Mr. ROHRABACHER. I see. So now we are in a global—they would not even have had to go to that Florida bank.

Mr. MOSCOW. Yes. We need to get everyone to cooperate.

Mr. ROHRABACHER. So right now, they would not have had to go to that Florida bank.

Mr. MOSCOW. Right.

Mr. ROHRABACHER. They could have been out of the Cayman Islands bank card.

Mr. WINER. If I may, the Treasury Department, in January, issued a new money laundering strategy in which they identified the need to deal with new payment systems, including stored value cards, debit cards, and to make sure that those kinds of payment systems have adequate safeguards in order to avoid them being used for money laundering, terrorist finance, and that kind of thing, and Treasury has announced that they are considering looking at a rulemaking soon to begin to address those kinds of issues. Those kinds of cards are used by populations that are not served by banks, and there is tremendous value to society in having those kinds of products available to people. There are also some risks and vulnerabilities that are going to have to be addressed.

Mr. EVANS. Mr. Chairman, the other thing that I think would be important is that you have a whole series of regulations and procedures now that the banks and many other financial institutions are following, but they are not universally applied across the Financial Services Committee. One of my colleagues mentioned the problem of hedge funds. They do not have any standards at all. There are many other financial institutions that are exempt for one reason or another just because nobody has gotten to it, and so the bad players will move to the lowest common denominator.

Mr. ROHRABACHER. I would like to look at the general issue of whether or not we can lead the world and set a standard, or whether or not we need to be, instead, trying to have a world standard as set by an international organization, meaning can we say, anyone doing business with American banks or any type of financial business within the United States is going to have to do this, or we are going to find ways of cutting you off from doing business with us until you meet that standard versus a protocol that is established internationally by an international institution.

Mr. GALLAGHER. Mr. Chairman, if I could point to the analogy of what happened a couple of years ago when a congressional Committee looked at correspondent banking, there was revolution effected simply by requiring that American banks denied correspondent facilities to foreign banks who went about their business in particular ways that were seen to be unsatisfactory.

That process worked remarkably smoothly, and I can tell you from my personal observation in the context of the Caribbean, it has done more to transform and clean up the act of the banks in the Caribbean than anything else because they are out of business if they cannot enjoy a correspondent relationship with a leading financial institution in the United States, simple as that.

Mr. ROHRABACHER. So if we use the authority that we have in order to control our own market and the way it is functioning, at least we can have some major progress in this area rather than having to wait for a protocol from the United Nations.

Mr. EVANS. But the unintended consequences can be purely competitive, if not done carefully and well, to simply drive business from American institutions to foreign institutions.

Mr. ROHRABACHER. Well, that is true of just about any regulation that you can talk about. We also have to figure out whether or not those other major financial leaders in the world see the threat of what we are trying to stop as being as important to them as it is to us. Mr. Moscow and then Mr. Winer. Mr. Moscow, go ahead.

Mr. MOSCOW. I was going to say that we have to persuade the other money centers in the world, and that means sitting down and talking with them and talking through the issues and getting them to agree. I am not suggesting that we need something as formalistic as the UN. It is a philosophy. We have to get people to understand that the ability to use money is the ability to exercise power, and we want the people who do that—we want to be able to hold them responsible, so we have to be able to trace the assets. We cannot go to London and say, gee, if we pass these regs, something else will happen. They will say, gee, we will get more business. We have to persuade them that London also has an interest in a world in which terrorism can be fought.

Mr. ROHRABACHER. All right. Mr. Winer?

Mr. WINER. Mr. Chairman, when I was at the State Department, I was dealing with this issue all of the time, and what I found was, like a good fighter, you need to be able to mix it up. The United States Government has used the Financial Action Task Force in Paris really very effectively through a series of Administrations now, going back to the first George Bush and continuing straight on through since, to get standards and norms in place globally which have been in U.S. interests.

Now, the Iran and Cuba counter-examples are important counter-examples, and in the Clinton Administration, we also from time to time did unilateral sanctions. For example, we put sanctions on Antigua before anyone else was really ready to do so, and it had an impact. It got Antigua to clean up its Russian bank problem pretty much immediately, though not some of the other ones that existed at the time.

So I would urge this Subcommittee to consider how to encourage the Administration, through its oversight and investigative functions, to mix it up, both to take advantage of international, multilateral modalities—forgive the dip speak—as well as mechanisms as well as organizations. FATF is really a modality or mechanism rather than an organization in the way in which it has functioned, as well as acting unilaterally. You need to do both.

Mr. ROHRABACHER. I am going to ask one more question and then go to Ms. Ros-Lehtinen. I just heard your answer to what I consider a core question of what we are looking at here today, but I want to come back with a follow-up that is based on a cynical analysis of the world, not to say necessarily that I have signed onto this cynical analysis.

When you say we have to talk to them and make sure they understand why these steps are necessary to get them to be responsible, is there not justification to think that perhaps these people are not going to understand because they do not want to be responsible because some of them are making huge amounts of money off of this, or am I mistaken that the financial community is just as clean as they look?

It is the guys who are robbing the local liquor stores who are the bad guys because they are getting away with that $65 out of the cash register, rather than these big financial institutions that are dealing in billions of dollars, and the people seem to be living in huge houses and lots of cars and living high on the hog. So why would they want to understand? Am I wrong? That is a cynical approach, and you are welcome to tear it down or build it up, whatever you would like.

Mr. EVANS. I would suggest the answer is probably in your questioning of the UBS representative.

Mr. MOSCOW. Rational persuasion comes in many forms, and there are some banks where CEOs, having been up on Capitol Hill, have sworn mighty oaths that they are never, ever going to do it again, and none of their employees are going to be permitted to act in a way that will cause them to be called up to the Hill again.

When you appeal to someone's better feelings, merely talking about good ideas is not the only way to get their attention.

Mr. ROHRABACHER. I see. So it relies on us in government to start getting tough. Again, you are going back to campaign finance laws.

Mr. WINER. When Mr. Moscow played a leading role in closing the bank of crooks and criminals international worldwide, VCCI Worldwide, the UK Government was sufficiently embarrassed that ultimately it completely changed its regulatory system to create the

Financial Services Authority and dramatically enhanced its ability to go after financial crime. That had an impact much more broadly.

Enforcement action, which Congress can stimulate and press for, makes a tremendous difference. When you pay a $100 million fine, that does tend to get somebody's attention, and it is not something they are going to want to do again. The shareholders will not like it.

Mr. GALLAGHER. Mr. Chairman, could I add to what Jonathan is saying in terms of penalties? The answer is not $100 million worth of fines or $200 million worth of fines. The answer is to hold the directors of the entity concerned personally liable and send them to jail. We have a structure in place for pursuing many of these matters which is administrative and civil. It needs to be taken out of that framework and put into the criminal framework. It is theft, one way or another.

Mr. ROHRABACHER. Here we are back to the original testimony.

Mr. GALLAGHER. And I think until we see a shift in the framework away from this notion of civil penalties and into a framework of criminal penalties, we are going to continue with the problem.

Mr. ROHRABACHER. Do you all agree with that?

Mr. EVANS. No.

Mr. ROHRABACHER. Okay.

Mr. EVANS. And I will tell you why. The burden of proof is much higher under criminal penalties. Under civil penalties, it is an easier burden, and we can get the bad guys easier civilly than they can criminally.

Mr. ROHRABACHER. All right. Ms. Ros-Lehtinen, would you like to take a final 1 minute here? All right. With Congress, when we are talking about who is going to set the standards, somebody has to get tough first, and who to get tough on, of course, and I mentioned campaign contributions. Whether it is campaign contributions, it is the attention that people want, and when the public demands a certain level of attention, this will get done, and hopefully this set of hearings that we are initiating today will get the public's attention and begin a discussion on this, so that we will have constituents who are not only concerned about what is going on in their own district, but constituents who are concerned about how we have international financial institutions that are being manipulated and run and being used as vehicles for all kinds of very evil behavior in this world.

Whether or not we get at it through a regulatory type of approach or a criminal type of approach, we will have that discussion as this goes on. I am going to give each one of you 1 minute to summarize what you think, and then we will be done with the hearing.

Mr. GALLAGHER. Well, could I just reaffirm your point and emphasize the fact that in many of these instances there is a conspiracy at the heart of the problem? In my book, the banker is every bit a part of the conspiracy as the criminals he is supporting, and he ought to go to jail at the same time they do.

Mr. ROHRABACHER. It is interesting. We started with that and ended with that, and I think that is a good place——

Mr. EVANS. Speaking as a retired banker, I agree with that. The bad players need to be driven out of the industry. But the key to so much of this is the international sharing of information and not just the sharing of information but the sharing of it quickly and expediently and enthusiastically, not having to extract every bit of information through a long legal process, and to that end, the more we can see in terms of international cooperation and international treaties that will facilitate that, I think that is all a good thing, not in lieu of anything else.

Mr. ROHRABACHER. Mr. Gallagher wants to say we are going to find these guys, we are going to treat them like criminals, and then the other guys are going to be afraid that they are going to be put in the poky, and so they will not do it. Your approach would be to let us establish standards like, for example, what we have talked about in terms of transparency, where every account is identified. Even if it takes a long time, the same account is identified as to who is involved in that account, and anybody who does not do that accurately will be held accountable for being a bad businessman and be fined and be dealt with as someone who has violated a regulation rather than as a criminal.

Mr. EVANS. Well said, Mr. Chairman. Do not misunderstand my point. I would love to see a criminal prosecution successfully pursued; they are just tougher than the civil——

Mr. ROHRABACHER. You are saying that the approach that you described that I just analyzed would be a much more effective way of getting change in a much quicker way. Yes, sir?

Mr. MOSCOW. Really quickly, I like the criminal prosecution, obviously, on the occasions when you can do it. I like the idea of holding the banks civilly liable to the person whose funds they are transmitting. In other words, if they know it is stolen funds, the British now have case law saying there is a civil trust imposed. So if they pay it over to Habacha's sons, and it came from the Central Bank of Nigeria, the bank could be liable for all of the money they transported. Hey, you had a trust. If you gave it away, that is your problem. You still have to give it back to the victim. That will tend to get attention.

The one point that I think needs to be made is that we have banks that are very, very large where there is a lot of regulatory and political pressure not to prosecute criminally because it would close them. I have been involved in the decision to prosecute banks and not to prosecute banks, and under the current circumstances, there is a limitation on criminal prosecutions, both in evidence and in terms of the collateral consequences because you have one or two groups of people committing crimes, and yet you have an institution worth $60 or $100 or $200 billion. You do not want to close it because of that.

Mr. ROHRABACHER. I see. So, in other words, if you do have one or two employees or someone who works for a financial institution who are committing a crime, no one else in the institution, including the stockholders—understand that—they can be held accountable and sent to jail, but why have the entire institution be damaged dramatically?

Mr. MOSCOW. It gets awkward when there is a lot of criminal behavior at senior levels in an institution that large, and there are such cases, and the problem of what to do with them is an open problem.

Mr. DELAHUNT. Enron.

Mr. ROHRABACHER. Mr. Winer?

Mr. WINER. Yes. Enron did use classic money laundering techniques, including some of the classic jurisdictions.

Thirty years ago, the Congress passed the Foreign Corrupt Practices Act, and 10 years ago, the European Union, the OECD countries came along and said, we are going to criminalize corruption and bribery, too. But it was only with the enactment of the Sarbanes-Oxley Act that you actually saw much in the way of Foreign Corrupt Practices Act cases, and the Justice Department is now seeing them every day of the week as a result of self-reporting by companies due to the requirements for certification by the CFOs, the CEOs, that the Sarbanes-Oxley Act has put into place.

Now, that has been partially globalized through American depository receipts. Foreign companies that are traded on the New York Stock Exchange have to sign up for the same thing. The further globalization of those standards would continue to facilitate financial transparency and integrity, and, again, market access issues. The price people are willing to pay for market access to the United States can be very, very substantial. People want it, and they are willing to do things and give up things in order to get it.

Mr. ROHRABACHER. Let me note for the record, although I am considering everything that you have said, that there are so many medium-sized businessmen that have come to me since Sarbanes-Oxley just telling me that they are being driven out of business, they no longer can operate. This has been horrendous. I do not know if it has anything to do with the part of the bill that you are talking about, but maybe there is another aspect of Sarbanes-Oxley that makes it——

Mr. WINER. There is an interesting question as to whether Sarbanes-Oxley could be tailored to provide for lower compliance costs for smaller businesses through less frequent audits, for example, biannual rather than annual, and there are a variety of other things which the SEC (Securities and Exchange Commission) has been looking at.

I would just note that there has been an impact on Foreign Corrupt Practices Act investigations, prosecutions, and cases resolved as a result of it, and it has had an impact even beyond the United States. So it is for Congress rather than for mere witnesses to balance out those issues.

Mr. ROHRABACHER. Yes, sir.

Mr. DELAHUNT. But with your good counsel, I guess, is the point.

Mr. ROHRABACHER. I am at the end, and I would be happy to let you, Mr. Delahunt, proceed, and then we will call an end to the hearing.

Mr. DELAHUNT. Okay. You know, I share the same experience that the Chairman has in terms of complaints about Sarbanes-Oxley, and I think that there is validity to those concerns, and yet I think the suggestion—I think it was you, Mr. Winer—that indicated there ought to be a review to determine whether it is feasible to secure a compliance regimen that is less costly for medium-sized and small business. But I think, I dare say, that what we are seeing as a result is more accountability because individuals are on the hook, and I think that is what, Mr. Moscow, you are talking about when we talked about trusts and subsidiaries and corporations.

It is so easy to hide. If there is a name associated and held accountable, that provokes a totally different response. I do not know how to go about that, but I dare say, and clearly in terms of criminal prosecution, you are sitting there, when you are bringing down seven-, eight-, nine-figure incomes a year, you are going to make damn sure that you are going to exit that position, you know, in a way that you can spend that kind of capital that you have acquired.

I think the point that you made, Mr. Moscow, and I am sure it does not come as any surprise to you that we really do not know what we are doing here. Okay? This is a very arcane issue. It really requires a level of expertise. Much of what we are hearing is Money Laundering 101, and there is a large learning curve not just simply for Members of this panel but, I dare say, Members of the Financial Services Committee, but it is really essential, I believe, to stay focused on increasing transparency and accountability to achieve, I think, what everybody wants to achieve. Maybe the ultimate legacy of Enron will be a more transparent, global, international system of finance. I guess there is a silver lining in every dark cloud.

Why is the Treasury so slow in terms of promulgating these rules and regulations? Look at the body English, Mr. Chairman. I have to ask these questions——

Mr. WINER. Congressman Delahunt, it is very important for experts to be able to maintain their nonpartisan expertise.

Mr. DELAHUNT. I understand that.

Mr. WINER. And, therefore, I would prefer not to answer the question for that reason, but I would point out that, generally speaking, Treasury has been underresourced for many, many years, and the ideological opposition and hostility to these issues, which was evident at Treasury, more or less changed in the middle of the Clinton Administration, not at the beginning, in the middle. It changed in the Bush Administration after the first year; that is, in the first 9 months, there was hostility toward this area of regulation. It flipped after the September 11, and since then, while there is support in principle for it, there has not been adequate resource allocation.

Mr. DELAHUNT. I really appreciate that answer. In addition to that and putting it in a nonpartisan way, I think it is a cheap investment. That is the bottom line. Then we would get a real return on our investment that would save—I just perused one of your—maybe it was a memorandum prepared by staff, but $6–7 trillion and illegal 600 to $1.5 trillion. We could have a lot of OFAC folk running around, and maybe it is a reorienting of our priorities, but I am not going to continue to ask questions, but if anyone has any further comments.

Mr. EVANS. Just to amplify what my colleague, Mr. Winer, was saying, that is true not only at Treasury, but the agencies that we work a great deal with, whether it is the SEC or the FTC (Federal Trade Commission), that are involved in this money laundering recovery, whatever you want to call it, they are all underresourced. They are all really stretched hard, and it is counterproductive.

Mr. DELAHUNT. Right. If there is no one there to answer the phone, then we can get up here, and we can make all sorts of statements about this bank and that bank and what we are going to do and all of those things, but you know what? It is our responsibility. We are not providing the resources to do the kind of investigations, and it is all sham and hot air. That is the bottom line.

Mr. ROHRABACHER. Is there any type of incentive system that we could provide? You uncover this much money laundering, you recovered so much that you are going to get to keep 10 percent or something like that. Is there something like that in the system already?

Mr. WINER. QUTAM.

Mr. ROHRABACHER. Is there a reward for people working with the government who uncover this, forfeiture laws?

Mr. GALLAGHER. It goes to the government.

Mr. ROHRABACHER. Yes. It goes to the government.

Mr. WINER. For example, there are terrorist reward programs which have been used in connection with some money laundering cases, I believe. I know somebody who is waiting for his reward, having gotten a terrorist financier in. So there are some problems.

Mr. ROHRABACHER. I think that if I could just ask you fellows to think of a way to put that type of incentive into the law and give me some personal recommendations on how you could incentivize people inside the bureaucracy and outside to find the bad guys and maybe with resulting prosecutions and any type of return, that a certain amount of money would go to the person responsible for bringing the information or responsible for that case, maybe we could get some action.

Mr. WINER. Mr. Chairman, I want to make one suggestion right here and now, which is if government agencies were able to convert some of the funds that were forfeited——

Mr. ROHRABACHER. Yes.

Mr. WINER [continuing]. Into FTE, into personnel, full-time equivalents, people who would be inside over a career rather than contractors or other purposes,——

Mr. ROHRABACHER. That is a good first step.

Mr. WINER [continuing]. That would be something which I think, over time, could strengthen——

Mr. ROHRABACHER. Listen, that is a very good suggestion and beyond. If there are some suggestions how to incentivize individuals inside and outside the government, I would be very happy to look at that and go see my good friend, Chris Cox, and we will see what we can do there.

Mr. EVANS. I would suggest also one of the incentives, at least from the banking community perspective, would be to have actual prosecutions happen more. The bankers are really tired of making a criminal referral with known bad guys, and then somebody at the FBI (Federal Bureau of Investigation) will say, off the record, "We cannot be quoted on this," but we just do not have the resources. This is not a big enough crime to go after.

Mr. DELAHUNT. I can remember the regulations. When I was the District Attorney in the greater Boston area, they would send them by the car load.

Mr. EVANS. You have got to pick and choose.

Mr. DELAHUNT. The resources demand that you pick and choose, so people are getting away with it. If we do not do the resourcing, then all we are doing is blowing hot air.

Mr. ROHRABACHER. If we follow Mr. Winer's advice, the more successful you are, the more resources you will have and be able to go after the bad guys.

Mr. DELAHUNT. You know, what I would suggest, Mr. Chairman, is that we think about, for lack of a better term, some sort of task force. You should communicate with the Speaker, and I could communicate with the Minority Leader, about putting a task force together comprised of some Members of the International Relations Committee with the Financial Services Committee to sit down with individuals like this who can bring some real-life experience and give us some guidance as to what you need.

It is clear to me that this really does require aggressive action by the Department of State and by the White House to say, hey, this is the way it has to be. We have, again, the carrot of market access, and when we have—what is the name of that country, Vanatatu?——

Mr. EVANS. Vanuatu.

Mr. DELAHUNT [continuing]. I mean, you could put them out of business.

Mr. ROHRABACHER. Okay. Now, has anybody here been in Vanuatu?

Mr. EVANS. I have, Mr. Rohrbacher.

Mr. ROHRABACHER. So have I. I have been to Vanuatu. That is very interesting. You should see. They have a little called Ray——

Mr. DELAHUNT. Do they have sting rays?

Mr. ROHRABACHER [continuing]. Sting rays that come up. No, they do not. I am just kidding you.

Anyway, with that said, I would like to thank the panel and thank all of the witnesses today, thank Mr. Delahunt, and I think this has been a very provocative hearing and one from which I have learned a lot. This is hopefully the first step in a series of hearings to be conducted on——

Mr. DELAHUNT. I am waiting for the magic words, Mr. Chairman.

Mr. ROHRABACHER [continuing]. And at some point, we will hold the final hearing, and by then we will see if Halliburton has actually snuck into the hearing.

Mr. DELAHUNT. I do not want to talk about Halliburton, but the issue of—we are talking about banking, and I understand—let us be very candid—we had to get UBS in here because of a political agenda. I understand that. I am not naive. Yet at the same time, I know that we have the responsibility, and we will not call it Halliburton, but there are subsidiaries of American companies that I would suggest are doing far more damage in terms of national security interests by going through sham corporations and sham trusts in dealing with our allies who are doing business in Iran in a joint venture way that makes it all a joke. Everybody knows it is happening, and we end up looking like hypocrites, and that is hurting us.

Mr. ROHRABACHER. Being another issue, we will discuss that publicly and privately in the future, in terms of this hearing, it was the opening of a series of hearings on the international financial institutions and the way they operate and whether or not different changes could be made that would be in the interest of the United States and world stability and just honesty in a global perspective.

So we appreciate all of you for participating in this first set of hearings, and I hope you will follow these hearings as they go along, and, again, I would like you to feel comfortable in putting something down, an idea on a piece of paper—here is my one-page summary of an idea that you might be able to put into the system, like you just said, forfeiture that would go directly to putting new investigators on when you get a good bust or something like that—that is a good idea and things like that that you might think that would energize the system.

So thank you all very much. This hearing is adjourned.

[Whereupon, at 5:12 p.m., the Subcommittee was adjourned.]

○

APEX
TP
*9780160765995*
76901953-4